JOEL McCREA
RIDING THE HIGH COUNTRY

Books by Tony Thomas

The Films of Errol Flynn (with Rudy Behlmer and Cliff McCarty)
The Busby Berkeley Book
Ustinov in Focus
Music for the Movies
Cads and Cavaliers
The Films of Kirk Douglas
Song and Dance: The Films of Gene Kelly
The Films of the Forties
Burt Lancaster
The Films of Marlon Brando
Hollywood's Hollywood (with Rudy Behlmer)
Harry Warren and the Hollywood Musical
Gregory Peck
The Great Adventure Films
The Films of 20th Century-Fox (with Aubrey Solomon)
Film Score
From a Life of Adventure
Ronald Reagan: The Hollywood Years
Hollywood and the American Image
The Films of Olivia de Havilland
The Films of Henry Fonda
That's Dancing
The Cinema of the Sea
James Stewart: A Wonderful Life
Howard Hughes in Hollywood
The West That Never Was
The Best of Universal
The Spy Who Never Was

JOEL McCREA
RIDING THE HIGH COUNTRY

by Tony Thomas

Riverwood Press, Burbank

Acknowledgments

My primary source of research for this book was provided by the library of The Academy of Motion Picture Arts and Sciences, Los Angeles. As on previous occasions, I am sincerely grateful for the help given me by Linda Mehr and her staff. I was thus able to supplement my own interviews with Joel McCrea with the many files on his life and films contained in the Academy library.

In illustrating the book I am indebted to John Lebold; Eddie Brandt's Saturday Matinee; Mark Willoughby of Collectors Book Shop, Hollywood; Bob Colman of Hollywood Poster Exchange; Neil Summers; Ray Pence of Jerry Ohlinger's Movie Store; Steve Sally and Karl Thiede, who also compiled the "Wichita Town" supplement. Without such help the book would not have been possible.

Tony Thomas
Joel McCrea, Riding The High Country

ISBN 1-880756-00-5

Riverwood Press
Burbank, California

Book designed by Sheridan Ryder

First Printing — January 1992

PRINTED IN THE UNITED STATES OF AMERICA

CONTENTS

JOEL McCREA - Metro-Goldwyn-Mayer

MGMP-12428

6

JOEL McCREA
RIDING THE HIGH COUNTRY

It is doubtful if any film actor has ever summed up a long career more modestly, more succinctly or more accurately than Joel McCrea: "I did the best I could—without trying too hard." In view of his having starred in eighty films over a thirty-year period during what is generally regarded as Holly-wood's Golden Age, it is a remarkably modest summation. His is an extraordinary filmography, one that has seldom been given much attention, possibly because McCrea himself was a man who never sought much attention. If it was his wish to avoid attention, he was successful because he is the most underrated of all the male stars of that Golden Age. His contemporaries—Gary Cooper, Clark Gable, James Stewart, John Wayne, Cary Grant, Spencer Tracy, James Cagney, Henry Fonda, Humphrey Bogart—have all been well assessed. Not so in the case of McCrea.

It is also doubtful if any other man as placid or as amiable as Joel McCrea ever became a major film figure. The words used to describe him do not usually appear in descriptions of movie stars: non-neurotic, non-egocentric, non-narcisistic. Ginger Rogers appeared with McCrea in two films and she once said of him, "One of the nicest, warmest, most generous-of-heart men in the world, he truly loves everybody. You have to have a very genuine love of humanity to risk having your feelings taken advantage of like this."

To describe McCrea only in terms of niceness is deceptive. The essential quality of McCrea as an actor was his strength. He was reliable, solid, sober, difficult to ruffle, dependable. And if he lacked much color he was at least likeable. Probably the harshest comment ever made about McCrea by a critic was the one which likened him to a concert pianist specializing in a single chord. What that critic might have missed was the art which conceals art.

Bryon Haskins, who directed McCrea in *The First Texan* (1956), told interviewer Joe Adamson: "I finally ran across the man I consider the greatest pure cinema actor I ever worked with - Joel Mc-Crea. I used to watch scenes on the set and think, Jesus, there wasn't anything to him - and I'd see him in the rushes the next day and it'd knock you off your seat, becuase of the hemming in of the camera on the sidelines, focused on McCrea..."

The essence of McCrea as an actor was his sense of realism. "I wasn't brilliant enough to take any kind of false position. I've always been a stickler for realism. I never was just an actor, I was more a personality. I played only parts I felt realistic in, or at least I did once I got to the point where I felt I had some say in the matter. When I was under contract to Sam Goldwyn I turned down a script he asked me to read. I said it was too good for me, I wasn't up to playing the role. He said, 'That's the

7

McCrea's first role — a one day job in the Marion Davies film **The Five O'Clock Girl** *(MGM 1929). William Randolph Hearst didn't like the film and prevented its release.*

first time I ever heard an actor say that.'"

Goldwyn was not the only producer or director surprised by McCrea's negative response to projects. When Warner's ace director Michael Curtiz was planning to film the story of Will Rogers, he approached McCrea knowing that Rogers had been not only a friend of the actor, but his idol. McCrea talked him out of the concept, explaining that all he would be able to do would be a poor imitation. He convinced Curtiz that he was unqualified and suggested Will Rogers, Jr., who was later hired.

"It never interested me enough to play parts I didn't feel at home in. For most of those years I was also making a living as a rancher so there was no incentive to do a film for any reason other than that I wanted to do it. I think we should be realistic about our abilities and adequacies, and expecially the lack of them. I never had an inferiority complex, I still asked for more money at the end of the year. It's just that I knew what I could and couldn't do. I often had people tell me that an actor should be able to play anything but I always argued with that. I said Leslie Howard was a marvelous actor but if he had tried to play Buffalo Bill it would have been silly. On the other hand I could play Buffalo Bill fairly easily and I wasn't anywhere near the actor Leslie was."

McCrea's modesty was that of a confident man, and one whose shrewdness was masked by an easy-going, seemingly guileless manner. It might well be that his success as a movie star had something to do with his success as a rancher and horseman. He ran a good ranch and he rode horses with skill and grace. That sense of grace marked him as a man.

One of the best assessments of Joel McCrea's image and success as a film actor is contained in James Harvey's book *Romantic Comedy* (Alfred A. Knopf, New York, 1987), which covers that Hollywood genre from Ernst Lubitsch to Preston Sturges. In comparing McCrea with Gary Cooper, the actor with whom McCrea is most often compared, Harvey doubts that McCrea could have played the roles Cooper did so well in the Frank Capra comedies, *Mr. Deeds Goes to Town* (1936) and *Meet John Doe* (1941). In Harvey's opinion McCrea was not a Capra type because, "He is too direct, too gruff even, and too lacking in self-consciousness. He is utterly imcapable of pathos of winsomeness." Harvey goes on to say that McCrea lacked the Cooper lambency, the art of running lightly and softly across the surface, and that unlike Cooper, McCrea's handsomeness had a slightly gimlet-eyed quality, "Appollo crossed with a small-town storekeeper...that paradox, however, is a clue to McCrea's complications. He is unflappably good-natured, for example, but alway with the threat of something erascible as well. In repose, he has an odd serene grumpiness. He is so self-contained and withdrawn at times that whatever feelings surface on his face tend to surprise us, though they're always convincing. He keeps us guessing in a lot of his films."

Hollywood is a mecca that has drawn its talent from every nook and cranny of the world. In the case of Joel McCrea it is not only a case of a local boy who made good but of one who never lived more that fifty miles from Hollywood. Joel Albert McCrea was born in South Pasadena on November 5, 1905, one of the two sons (and one daughter) of Lou Whipple and Thomas P. McCrea. Both parents came from pioneer stock. The maternal grandfather, Major Albert Whipple, came west with a wagon train in the mid-nineteenth century and established a hotel in San Francisco. The paternal grandfather, Major John McCrea, fought under under the command of General Phinneas Banning in the campaigns against the Apaches and later was involved in a stage coach line. Thomas became an executive with the Los Angeles Gas and Electric Company, now the Southern California Gas Company. After a promotion he moved his family to Hollywood in 1914, buying a piece of land on what is now the west end of Hollywood Boulevard at the point where it joins Nichols Canyon.

McCrea attended a public school on Gardner Street, about a mile to the east of his home. He rode a bicycle to school and around Hollywood to watch pictures being made. In 1916 he would cycle down Sunset Boulevard to watch D. W. Griffith shooting *Intolerance*. "They had the biggest set ever made, amazing in those days, and Griffith would sit there in his chair, wearing that hat he always wore, and he looked more romantic than the leading man. Years later I remember watching Rex Ingram making *The Four Horsemen of the Apocalypse*. They were wonderful times."

McCrea entered Hollywood High School in 1919, at a time when it was fashionable for people in the industry to allow their children to attend. Because of that he met many youngsters whose parents were movie performers, technicians or executives. In his last year Los Angeles was hit by the influenza epidemic and all schools were closed. Needing to get a record of attendance in order to qualify for college, McCrea was permitted to attend the private Hollywood School for Girls along with the likes of Douglas Fairbanks, Jr. and Jesse Lasky,

With Will Rogers and Peggy Ross, **Business and Pleasure** *(Fox 1931).*

Jr. In her book *Hollywood: When Silents Were Golden,* Evelyn F. Scott recalls the young Joel as, "a tall youth with a pleasant smile, though not the brilliant one we basked in later on. Perhaps the brilliance came from the reflection that the worst had already happened to him. It was not going to be easy to have on his record that he once attended a girls' school. Probably it wasn't even easy while he did. Down at my level, the shock of his presence was muted and delayed, but no one between the jacaranda and the castor beans could ignore the flutter of notebooks, bosoms and eyelashes. With the term ended, Joel was gone. He came into our lives again as the most gloriously tanned, agreeable and lithe of the many dazzling young men at the Santa Monica Beach Club. Watching Joel leap at the net for a 'kill' in the volleyball was as thrilling as watching a good surfer catch a wave."

The hobnobbing with people in the picture business began for McCrea before he set foot in Hollywood High School. His first job was as a newspaper boy at the age of nine. "My family was moderately well off but I always wanted to work and own my own things. Being Scotch-Irish my father was in favor of it." Among the newspaper boy's clients was Cecil B. DeMille, who appreciated the fact that the boy threw the paper directly on to

9

With Frances Dee in September 1933

njamin David Scott was a red-headed little Irishman and a terrific guy. I told him I wanted to be a rancher but he said that from my readings in class he thought I had some talent I should use. He said, 'You have ability and you're making a big mistake if you don't do something with it.' Then he pointed out that it would take me years to earn enough money to buy a ranch but that if I worked in the movies I might get there a lot faster. I took the advice."

Pomona provided McCrea with more and more opportunities to co-mingle with the movie people. One of his fellow students was DeMille's daughter Cecilia, and that would be a point in his favor in the not too distant future. Pomona College, picturesquely situated in hilly country halfway between Pasadena and San Bernadino, was occasionally used as a location for college films. One of them was *The Fair Co-Ed* in 1927 with Marion Davies. It was student McCrea, wearing blond wig and red dress, who doubled for her in a riding sequence. He got the job because the previous year he had done a similar stunt for Greta Garbo in *The Torrent*. On that occasion "Someone threw a woman's cloak over my shoulder and another yelled 'action!' and off I rode through the woods as Garbo. After it was finished she came up to me on her horse and thanked me. I think she took a shine to me, until she asked, 'What do you want to do in films?' I answered that I wanted to be an actor. With that she said, 'Too bad. I don't like actors.'"

Another somewhat daunting comment came from serial queen Ruth Roland. While out riding during a summer break, McCrea came across her company on location. The leading man was balking at having to do a stunt requiring him to climb down a cliff on a rope, jump to a rock and then leap onto a horse. McCrea remarked that the the stunt looked easy to him, whereupon the director offered him two dollars and fifty cents to put on the leading man's clothes and do it. Afterwards Ruth Roland, who admired the young man's horsemanship, advised him to "Keep out of this film acting business, your chances are too slim."

At Pomona College, under the guidance of Benjamin David Scott, McCrea played leads in plays like *The Patsy* and *The Little Journal*, and character parts in *To the Ladies* and *Loyalties*. One of the girls in *The Patsy* was Jeane Wood, whose father was the director Sam Wood. She introduced McCrea to her father. Wood later decided to film *The Fair Co-Ed* at Pomona and offered McCrea work as an extra and as a double for the stunt involving Marion Davies.

the porch when it rained, and later gave him a silver dollar as a token of his regard. That coin would be of help later. Among his other customers was wealthy meat-packer tycoon J. P. Cudahy, whose twelve-year-old son Michael envied McCrea's breezy career delivering papers. In return for his letting Michael accompany him on his route, McCrea was invited to the Cudahy home where he sometimes met movie stars. One of them happened to be McCrea's hero, William S. Hart. Years later the two would become friends and it has often been said that McCrea's style as an actor, particularly in westerns, shows the influence of Hart.

It was while attending the Hollywood School for Girls that McCrea had his first theatrical experience. He did bits in plays, one of which featured young Harleen Carpenter, who soon became known as Jean Harlow. But none of the plays or the contact with picture people instilled in McCrea any desire to be an actor. During the summers he worked as a stableboy in local riding schools, as a hand on ranches and later as a teamster. His mind was already set on ranching, and it continued to be when he enrolled in Pomona College in 1924.

At Pomona McCrea attended, for no specific reason, courses in public speaking and in drama. He thought nothing about it until the head of the Drama Department called him in for an interview. "Be-

Getting to know the friendly and generous Davies was another step in the right direction for McCrea. She introduced him to her celebrated protector-lover William Randolph Hearst, which resulted in McCrea's later visits to the Hearst Castle at San Simeon. Also the fact that Davies was making her films at MGM provided a useful doorway.

McCrea graduated from Pomona in the Spring of 1928 and bagan his attack on the motion picture industry. He found that merely knowing famous and influential people is no guarantee of employment. However, work as an extra was fairly easy to come by. Joining him in what is called "the human furniture business" were friends like Jean Harlow, Carole Lombard and Jeane Wood, who would find success as K. T. Stevens. They all turned up for any chance to be tested for a film role. "As I recall, the directors always told us that we had promise but needed experience. We were determined to get it and bombarded Central Casting. There never seemed to be any roles but there was always an opportunity to test at one studio or another, which was experience of a kind."

By early 1929 things began to open up for McCrea. He danced with Greta Garbo in a ballroom scene in *The Single Standard*, for which he was paid sixteen dollars. A few major tests now came his way. He was considered for *The Big Trail*, but Fox decided instead on the unknown John Wayne. He tested for *Liliom* but lost to his friend Charles Farrell.

Then Sam Wood, doubtless with his daughter's encouragement, gave McCrea a note of introduction to Gloria Swanson. She was impressed enough to send him to producer William LeBaron at FBO, which was about to merge with RKO. LeBaron signed him at one hundred dollars a week and gave him a small part in *The Jazz Age*, starring his school chum Douglas Fairbanks, Jr. In this film about civic corruption McCrea played a spoiled playboy and did it so poorly that the studio offered him nothing else. At this point Sam Wood gave McCrea a bit as a student in *So This is College*, which was made at MGM where Cecil B. DeMille was then based.

Cecil B. DeMille was casting *Dynamite* and was testing many young actors for the roles in those parts of the film which dealt with college and life in society. "I went into his office. He had three secretaries, who all said I couldn't see Mr. DeMille, even though I claimed I knew him and had been to his home. I said I'd wait. When he came out to go to lunch he recognized me—I'd dated Cecelia several times—and he asked me what I wanted. I said I'd

Chance at Heaven *(RKO 1933)*

heard he was making his first talkie and since I'd done school plays I thought I'd be good for a part. He told me to come into his office, and when I came out I had a contract for a hundred bucks a week and a part in *Dynamite*. I guess telling him I still had the silver dollar he had given me as a newsboy didn't hurt."

The role of Marco, the playboy friend of a married lady, did not bring McCrea the MGM contract he had expected. He made little impression on the front office. "I'll never forget the day they let me go. An executive called me into his office and told me that they had Johnny Mack Brown and James Murray under contract, and that they were concentrating on them among the younger actors. It was still an era of medium-sized heroes and at six-foot-three I looked like the community flagpole. He suggested that I retire from pictures, wait until I was a bit older, and then do character parts, like Ernest Torrence. 'But how,' I asked him, 'am I going to eat until I'm as old as Ernest Torrence?' That stumped him too, and I left without the matter being resolved."

RKO Radio Pictures came into being in 1929, with the Radio-Keith-Orpheum Corporation absorbing the FBO Studio. William LeBaron was made Head of Production and he thought about McCrea when *The Silver Horde* was up for casting. McCrea's contract with FBO had not been formally terminated and his name came up for consideration for the roster of films RKO planned. The Rex Beach adventure story set in the Alaskan fishing industry called for a young man as the lead, and one who could talk, which was then an industry concern. "Everyone in town was scared to death of talkies. I remember John Gilbert asking me, 'Can you talk?' I laughed and said I'd been doing it for years. I wasn't an actor yet and I didn't have sense enough to be scared. I had a fair voice, and so I came in on the wave of the talkies."

A considerable factor in McCrea being chosen as the leading man in *The Silver Horde* was that William Randolph Hearst mentioned the young man's name in asking his friends at RKO how things were proceeding. McCrea had made several visits to San Simeon by this time, where the ever friendly Marion Davies often boosted the careers of yound actors she felt needed help. In 1929 the blessings of Hearst and Davies were not of minor value, and with the success of *The Silver Horde* the film career of Joel McCrea was off and running.

Someone else of great importance was about to come into McCrea's life—Will Rogers. Now under contract to RKO, the fledgling actor was loaned to Fox to play the romantic lead in Roger's *Lightnin'*. Rogers looked at a number of actors on film and decided on McCrea. They met for the first time when they were on location near Lake Tahoe and the two became instant friends. "He was almost like a father figure to me, and he taught me a lot about humility. He was a great humanitarian and I went along with his philosophy, and he's the one who instigated my buying a ranch when I did. He knew I wanted one but I would probably have waited ten years and saved up the money to get it. Will said, 'No. Go borrow some money and buy it. Land in California can't go any place but up.' He was right. When I sold off most of the land years later I made more money that I had in thirty years of making pictures."

It was while making his second film with Will Rogers, *Business and Pleasure* in 1932, that McCrea got around to making his move. With $4600 he purchased one thousand acres of land in the Santa Rosa Valley in the area between Moorpark and Camarillo, some forty miles west of Los Angeles. There he built a ranch house that would be his home from then on. "Will told me, 'You need to get out of this town regularly to get perspective on it, and there's no better spot than the back of a horse, herdin' cows.' He was right." McCrea stocked his ranch with cattle, and planted the fields with oats and barley. In time he added to the property, and also bought ranches in northern California, Nevada and New Mexico. At its peak in the early Fifties the Santa Rosa ranch covered four square miles and ran three hundred head of cattle. At the same time it produced thousands of bushels of barley, which McCrea sold at three dollars per bushel.

In 1931 RKO renegotiated McCrea's contract, retaining him for the next four years and used him mostly as a leading man to all their top leading ladies. First came Constance Bennett in *Once a Sinner* and she liked him so much she opted to appear with him in three of her later films. While no critics ever raved about his acting, it nonetheless brought him a reputation as a thoroughly reliable and believable foil for the likes of Bennett, her sister Joan, Irene Dunne, Barbara Stanwyck, Dolores Del Rio, Ginger Rogers, Kay Francis, Ginger Rogers, Claudette Colbert, Miriam Hopkins and Jean Arthur. For an actor still in his twenties McCrea could hardly complain about exposure, although he did begin to complain about the kind of pictures in which he found himself cast, especially those for which RKO loaned him to other studios. In 1931 he

appeared in five films, six in 1932 and four in 1933. He would average three per year for the remainder of the decade.

The relaxed manner was one upon which McCrea decided almost from the start. "I learned in those early years of being an extra and a bit player that it didn't pay to press too hard. Better to be content. But I fortified myself by watching the great screen talents at work. I analyzed the reasons for their success and I discovered the one quality common to all of them—poise. People ask me how I remain calm in the face of difficulties and I quote something the great actor George Arliss once said to me, 'What other than a pair of trousers can you improve by pressing?'"

While many of the parts McCrea played during the Thirties were not of great interest they were at least ones in which he seldom felt uncomfortable. "I managed to get out of those I knew I couldn't handle. In those first ten years I was paired with actresses who were much more important than me, like Connie Bennett and Irene Dunne. I would go to them and say, 'You know, I don't have a clue as to what this thing is about. I've got to be honest with you. I just worked on a ranch and I was a cowboy, and I don't really know anything...' That would scare them a little. So they would then work on my side in getting me out of these things and getting Cary Grant or Robert Montgomery to do them."

One film in which McCrea was uncomfortably stuck was *The Devil is a Woman*, starring Marlene Dietrich and directed by Josef von Sternberg, with whom Dietrich had already made a half dozen of her most successful films. McCrea was loaned to Paramount by RKO for the role of a Spanish political refugee in a story set in Seville in 1890. McCrea worked only one day. After forty-seven takes on his first scene he walked off and refused to return. It was the only time in his career that he took such an action. He hated the part, which eventually went to Cesar Romero, thinking himself totally unqualified to play a Spaniard. In point of fact McCrea never played any part other than an American, and the only period costumes he ever wore were those required for his westerns, which were mostly set in the late nineteenth century.

While making *The Silver Cord* at RKO in 1933, McCrea met Frances Dee, who had been borrowed from Paramount to play the secondary female role. The attraction, each for the other, was immediate and a courtship was soon in progress. Following his next film, *Bed of Roses*, with Constance Bennett, McCrea and Dee were paired by RKO in *One Man's*

By the pool at his ranch near Camarillo, California.

Journey. Dee then asked Paramount to release her from her contract, which enabled her to sign one with RKO. She and McCrea were married in Rye, New York, on October 20, 1933.

Frances Dee was born in Los Angeles on November 26, 1907. At one period during their childhood, she and McCrea had lived within a few blocks of each other, although they never met. She moved with her family to Chicago, where she excelled in school plays. Moving back to California she enrolled in the prestigious Pasadena Playhouse, the crucible of a great amount of Hollywood talent. She made her film debut doing a bit in the Fox film *Words and Music* (1929), in which John Wayne also had a bit. Paramount signed her to a contract and by the time she met McCrea, Dee had appeared in a dozen films, most notably *An American Tragedy* and *Rich Man's Folly*, both in 1931. Once under contract to RKO she won critical and public approval with her work in such films as *Little Women* (1933), *Of Human Bondage* (1934) and *Becky Sharp* (1935). It was a flourishing career but one she seconded to that of being Mrs. Joel McCrea and becoming a mother.

Jody, the first of the three McCrea sons, was born September 6, 1934, with David arriving on November 15, 1936. Almost twenty years later came Peter,

14

born on Easter Sunday in April of 1955. McCrea recalls that not long after this unplanned extension to the family he was a guest on a television talk show. "The hostess asked me, 'How did that happen?' I couldn't think of anything in reply that could be spoken on the air. I haven't been on any talk shows since then."

While expecting her first son Frances Dee asked to be released from her RKO contract. She cut back on her film appearances, making about one film each year until her last in 1954, *Gypsy Colt*. Her peak film year was in 1937, when she signed with Paramount for three films: *Souls at Sea*, with Gary Cooper, *Wells Fargo*, with her husband, and *If I were King*, with Ronald Colman, released in 1938. Her admirers believe that she was never more beautiful or more effective than in that group of three excellent movies.

Looking back on the people who have most influenced his life, McCrea claims that short of his father, Will Rogers had the most effect. "He was a man of such integrity and such sanity and dignity that it was an example you had to be stupid not to follow." Another man he admired was Gary Cooper, not simply as a friend but as a man of principle. "Coop was very shy, much more so than I was, but that was part of his charm, especially to the

The McCreas attending a wartime benefit, Decemeber, 1941.

ladies. We spent a lot of time together before each of us was married, going out together and double-dating. After he married I didn't see so much of him because his wife Rocky was very social, and I wasn't. I wasn't actually anti-social, it was just that I never much liked the Hollywood social life. But I used to watch him work and that was a kind of influence. He was quiet and sincere and I always felt that he stayed within his bounds. But I never copied him. It's a disaster to copy. I also used to watch John Barrymore and Paul Muni, and I admired them very much. I never even tried to copy my idol, William S. Hart. I liked him better than Tom Mix because although Mix was colorful Hart was sincere. He thought everything he did on the screen was real, he was great on authenticity and I admired that. But with Coop I watched him to see his approach to things, how honest he was, and then I tried to be honest in my own way and not go beyond my bounds."

McCrea's greatest praise was reserved for his wife. "She gave me my greatest sense of responsibility, and we stayed sane. Our backgrounds helped. No one in my family was in show business or the professions, and with that kind of background you're inclined to look at things more realistically. Frances was a very talented actress but once the children came along the family came first. She's very strong. I was inclined to walk away when things got tough but not her. Frances is a sticker-outer. That's been a tremendous help to me and an influence. I wasn't bright enough not to have gone awry occasionally, but the kind of relationship we had, the kind of marriage, has made it possible for me to rise to the occasion when I had to. You wouldn't think to look at that delicate, fragile beauty of hers but she's one of the strongest human beings I've ever known."

The McCrea career took a major step forward in 1936 when he was signed to a contract by Samuel Goldwyn. *Barbary Coast* was the first of seven Goldwyn pictures in which he would star over the next three years. His stock in Hollywood was greatly increased with this move. McCrea, who could do a fair imitation of Goldwynian speech and manner, says, "Goldwyn was a very strange man in some ways but he loved making movies and he tried for quality. Some actors had trouble with him but he was good to me. He was also funny with his bizarre statements and the way he mangled people's names. He used to call Errol Flynn—Earl Flint. Me he called Joe McCreal. One day one of his executives tried to correct him and he snapped back,

'Who is it who is paying Joe McCreal three thousand dollars a week. Me or you?' So there was no arguing with him about language."

People found McCrea a man not likely to back down in arguments, especially anything having to do with ranching. Harry Warner, the Warner brother who looked after the books, found that in trying to sell a herd of cattle to McCrea he received no concession to his position as a powerful producer talking to an actor. The stubborn McCrea, a careful man with money, actually ended up paying Warner less than the going price. A similar stance was taken in dealing with the Internal Revenue Service. McCrea always listed his profession as Rancher, with Acting an avocation. The IRS took exception to this on one occasion and threatened to disallow his operating expenses on the ranch. McCrea wanted to know on what basis this decision was made. The agent referred to the case of a dentist who had deducted the expenses of his farm although he lived on it only two weeks a year and did none of the work himself. Stormed McCrea, "You're a little confused, mister. I live on this ranch, it's my only home. Santa Rosa is where I get my mail and where my boys went to school. I vote here and I pay my taxes here. As for working it, look at these hands. I didn't get these calluses from acting." The IRS backed down.

Although the Joel McCrea image in Hollywood history is now fixed as that of a westerner he did not appear in a western until *Wells Fargo* in 1937. Two years later he starred in Cecil B. DeMille's epic *Union Pacific*, but again it was considered as simply another role in a variety of films. In 1940 McCrea starred in Hitchcock's *Foreign Correspondent*, which proved to be a career advancement. Hitchcock had wanted Gary Cooper for the role of an American newspaperman reporting from Europe in the first year of the second World War, but Cooper turned it down, thinking it was simply a suspense thriller. He later said he regretted the decision, but not the fact that is had helped McCrea.

The next advancement in the McCrea career was a major one. Preston Sturges, who had been a writer at Paramount all through the Thirties, finally got the studio to allow him to direct his own material. *The Great McGinty* in 1940 triggered a string of successful Sturges comedies, with *The Lady Eve* the following year being hailed as a work of comic genius. Sturges next put into production a film which satirized the movie business, *Sullivan's Travels*, choosing McCrea to play John L. Sullivan, a film director with a passion to make serious movies

With Maureen O'Hara in **Buffalo Bill** *(20th Century-Fox 1944).*

instead of those that simply amuse. Sturges had known McCrea for years and later said how much he admired the actor's persona and the image of quiet determination. Sturges himself was a flamboyant personality, eccentric and wildly generous, but it might be that in McCrea he saw an aspect of himself as someone he would like to have been. Whatever it was it worked beautifully. Says McCrea, "We were great friends and I liked working with him. He was brilliant, and he wrote dialogue I could remember. He told me he had written the scripts with me in mind and that gave me confidence. I'd say, 'Nobody writes anything for me,' and he'd shake his head, 'I want you. You're the one.' With someone like me who's not too cocksure of himself that was the kind of compliment I needed. It gave me the strength to do what he wanted of me."

McCrea made two more films for Sturges. The first, *The Palm Beach Story*, was a success and the second, *The Great Moment*, a failure. The second, the story of Dr. W. T. G. Morton, the dentist who discovered anesthesia, was made in 1942 but not released until two years later, so uncertain was Paramount of the marketability of this strange comedy-drama. By the time it appeared McCrea had scored a hit with George Stevens' classic wartime comedy *The More the Merrier*. Also *Buffalo Bill* had McCrea pleasing the public in a colorful but

McCrea, the working rancher, 1948.

With Veronica Lake in **Ramrod** *(United Artists 1947).*

none too accurate depiction of William F. Cody. Sturges' intention to use McCrea in several more films never came about; nothing that he did after *The Great Moment* called for the image of McCrea.

During the years of America's involvement in World War II McCrea appeared in only six films, remarkably few for any major film actor not engaged in military service. What is even more remarkable was his refusal to appear in any war films that would require the wearing of uniforms. Thirty-six at the time of the attack on Pearl Harbor, McCrea said, "If I was too old to be called, I was too old for that kind of film." It was a firm and unusual stand to be taken by a major star at a time when Hollywood was short of actors to play heroes in war movies. He was not, however, uninvolved in the war effort. As a beef-producing rancher he was asked to step up his productivity, which reached a high of some two hundred thousand pounds a year. There was also a good deal of talk about McCrea being given a post with the Department of Agriculture, but it never came about.

McCrea was approached by the government on another matter. "They asked me if I would tour the camps and hospitals. I said I had no talents as a dancer or singer, and that all I would be able to do is talk to the men. They said that was exactly what they wanted, some familiar faces to go around and chat with the fellows, especially those coming back wounded from overseas. That was something I could do, and did."

The postwar years brought many changes to Hollywood. The market began to change with the changes in public tastes and attitudes. Actors and directors and writers returning from war service came back with the desire to do films of a more realistic nature. This included westerns, which gradually became grittier and more honest in dealing with a West that had been virtually turned into American mythology by Hollywood. Joel McCrea was very much a part of that urge to make westerns for adults rather than entirely for the juvenile market.

With *The Virginian* in 1946, McCrea made a decision; from that point on he would specialize in westerns. "I wasn't instinctively an actor and I had no burning desire to act. but I liked making movies and I wanted to do the western things I had read about, like *The Virginian*, and different things like *Ramrod* and *Four Faces West*. I had enjoyed doing the comedies but as I got older I was better suited to westerns. The minute I got on a horse, with the hat and the boots, I felt easier. I didn't feel like I

17

Indian dialect is practiced with Nipo T. Strongheart and an Indian actor during the filming of **The Outriders** *(MGM 1950).*

was an actor anymore. I felt like the men I was playing.

"When I was doing Wyatt Earp in *Whichita* I believed in what I was doing. I studied the period. I had read Stuart N. Lake's book *Frontier Marshall* and I knew what Earp was thinking. I tried to be authentic about the West, and that wasn't hard for me because I was part of it. But the big advantage for me with westerns is that I could go on and on. When you're young it's all right to romance young ladies on the screen but not when you become mature."

Of the twenty-five films McCrea made between 1946 and 1959, only one, *Rough Shoot* (1953), was not a western. All of them were thoroughly professional films that easily returned their investments. A few, like **Colorado Territory** (1949), *Wichita* (1955) and *Fort Massacre* (1958) were exceptionally good and gave McCrea scope for strong characterizations. His knowledge of western life, of ranching, horses and cattle, obviously made Joel McCrea a believable presence in western movies.

In 1959 McCrea decided that it was time to bring his years as a moviemaker to an end. Four years

previously he had signed a contract with producer Walter Mirisch which resulted in six films, the last of which turned out to be the somewhat pedestrian *Gunfight at Dodge City*. Following that McCrea agreed to do a television series with Marisch, *Wichita Town*, a weekly half-hour for NBC. The great expectations of the network, the producer and the star were not met. After twenty-four episodes *Wichita Town* was cancelled. It was a time when televisions westerns were being produced in abundance, which was the main reason for McCrea's decision to stop making films. "These westerns we had been doing with Mirisch with budgets of about five hundred or six hundred thousand dollars were no longer drawing people into the theatres because they were sitting at home watching *Gunsmoke* with Jim Arness, which was then being turned out for around forty thousand dollars an episode, as was *Bonanza*. They were marvelous series, I enjoyed watching them myself. With *Wichita Town* failing to make much of an impression I thought it best to quit. I had nothing to prove, and I didn't need the money or the exposure."

The McCrea decision to retire was not absolute.

It was taken with an eye open in case anything really worthwhile came along. Nothing did until he received a phone call from Randolph Scott in 1961, saying that he had a script called *Guns in the Afternoon*, about a couple of old westerners down on their luck, and that McCrea might find it interesting. The two veterans had a meeting with producer Richard E. Lyons and director Sam Peckinpah, and out of it came one of the most honored of all western films, *Ride the High Country*. The title was apt—a pair of much admired movie westerners riding off into the sunset of long careers.

For Randolph Scott *Ride the High Country* was retirement absolute. A man of great wealth with multiple business concerns, nothing would induce him to return to picture making, or to have any further involvement with Hollywood life, of which he had never been much part anyway. Those who worked with the gentlemanly Scott noted that during breaks in filming he did not, as did most every other actor, read *Variety* or *The Hollywood Reporter*. He read *The Wall Street Journal*. McCrea again said he had entered retirement but allowed that there was always the possibility of considering a good script. "But nothing came along that I really liked. Most of it was kind of degrading stuff, sort of mangy. I didn't need that. I feel like the man I played in *Ride the High Country*. He said, 'All I want to do is enter my house justified.' So do I."

In 1970 Jody McCrea co-produced a western titled *Cry Blood, Apache*, a rather brutal account of gold miners killing both Indians and themselves with their greed, and he persuaded his father to play a small part. The film was a failure and afterwards Jody decided on the life of a rancher, as had his brother David who operated his own spread in New Mexico. Four years later McCrea agreed to be the narrator for Kieth Merrill's fine documentary *The Great American Cowboy*. Another two years went by before McCrea recieved a script he liked. The young Canadian producer-writer-director John Champion asked McCrea to come to Canada to play an old rancher who sets out in company with a young Indian boy to track a black stallion. *Mustang Country*, a somewhat Disneyesque wild life picture, did not find much of an audience and soon drifted into limbo. Doubtless this had something to do with McCrea's decision never to appear in another film.

Ever a shrewd businessman and sound investor, McCrea decided in 1959 to sell 540 of the 3000 acres occupied by his ranch near Camarillo, his original land purchase. Four years later he sold another

With 18 year old Jodie on location of **Border River** *(Universal 1954)*.

1000 acres for $3,000,000, while continuing to live on the remainder of the property. He also continued to supervise the operation of his 2600-acre ranch near San Luis Obispo and the two in New Mexico managed—and now owned—by his sons Jody and David. His son Peter opted to become a real estate developer rather than a rancher.

His strong western identity made it inevitable that McCrea be honored by election to The Cowboy Hall of Fame in Oklahoma City in 1958. The honor had much to do with his film image but the selection also took into consideration his standing as a solid citizen. McCrea served as president of his local school board, chaired fund raising committees, notably for the Camarillo Boys Club, and donated large sums of money to local colleges and the Tri-Valley YMCA. He gave parcels of land to nearby California Lutheran College, and he made grants to Claremont Graduate School, to his alma mater Pomona College and sundry charities, including scholarships for American Indians.

Musing upon his long film career McCrea said, "I guess I'm like some of the western characters I played, the image of *The Virginian*, something like that. I tried to be believable and authentic. That's where I had something to offer. I stayed within my scope more out of common sense than humility. Preston Sturges once told me that you had no right to drag people into a theatre and bore them. I tried not to be boring."

Joel McCrea was never boring, on or off the screen. And perhaps more than any other actor he was largely the same man on screen as off. He was always concerned about his screen image and he never compromised it. He sometimes played men confused in their values but he refused to portray villainy or to do or say anything of questionable taste in a film. He was a sensible man and he knew what was of value to him. He seemingly never forgot some advise given to him in his early career by *Los Angeles Times* columnist Harry Carr: "Don't let yourself slip into a state of mind where you believe that these little screen games of pretend are life. Take all the easy money and save it. Accept what you find in Hollywood that is good and valuable and turn your back on the rest."

The end came for Joel McCrea at 5:40 on the morning of October 20, 1990, seventeen days short of his eighty-fifth birthday. Two weeks prior he caught a cold which turned into influenza. He was taken to the Motion Picture and Television Fund Hospital in Woodland Hills, not far from his home and died a few days later from pulmonary complications. Frances, his wife of fifty-seven years, was with him all the time.

Joel McCrea was last seen in public three weeks before his death. He attended a Beverly Hills fund raising dinner for Senator Pete Wilson, then running as a Republican candidate for governor of California. The keynote speaker was Barbara Bush, who immediately after her speech went up to McCrea, put her hand in his and said, "My hero." With him was his friend of fifty years, the veteran Paramount film producer A.C. Lyles. "When Mrs. Bush said that to him he just lit up. He beamed. It was a touching moment, not just for him but for all of us who knew Joel because what she said summed up how we all felt about him. Joel was unique. He was a strong, kindly, good natured, decent, dignified man. I can truly say I never knew another quite like him."

The Films of Joel McCrea

DYNAMITE

MGM, 1929;
produced and directed by Cecil B. DeMille; written by Jeannie Macpherson, John Howard Lawson and Gladys Unger; photographed by J. Peverell Marley; music by Herbert Stothart; 14 reels.

Cast:
Cynthia Crowthers, Kay Johnson; *Hagon Derk*, Charles Bickford; *Roger Towne*, Conrad Nagel; *Marcia Towne*, Julia Faye; *Katie Derk*, Muriel McCormac; *Marko*, Joel McCrea

Cecil B. DeMille's first talking picture provided Joel McCrea with his first featured role—and opened the door to a long and pleasing career in the movie business. The twenty-four year old McCrea would no longer have to scurry about Hollywood

With Julia Faye.

trying to get into this or that film. From here on work was offered instead of sought.

By 1929, DeMille had established his reputation as Hollywood's most flamboyant producer-director. Starting with *The Squaw Man* in 1913, he had by the coming of sound made some fifty movies, ever more pictorially grandiose, dramatically ripe and floridly romantic. He had also proven that the Bible was a reliable source for such material, particularly with *The Ten Comandments* (1923) and *The King of Kings* (1927). The critics and the customers expected something along those lines for his first outing with sound. What they got instead was *Dynamite*, which was epic only in its length, with fourteen reels running over two hours. The setting of the film is contemporary high society, with the heroine marrying below her station, becoming involved in mining which allows for a lavishly staged mine cave-in as the climax.

The heroine is socialite Cynthia Crowthers (Kay Johnson) who marries miner Hagon Derk (Charles Bickford) in order to comply with the instructions contained in her father's will. This enables her to inherit a vast amount of money, after which she intends to marry the man she really loves, Roger Towne (Conrad Nagel); he is unhappily married to Marcia (Julia Faye), who whiles away her idle hours with her young lover known as Marco, the Sheik (McCrea). Playboy Marco is so called because he is regarded in society as little more than a gigolo. Cynthia imagines her problems have been solved when her husband is arrested for murder and condemned to die. However, he is exonerated and returns to the mine, and though she realizes he has a low opinion of her he agrees to take her with him.

Roger still loves Cynthia and follows her to the mining town. However, he soon realizes that he is interfering with a marriage and that Derk is not such a bad fellow after all. While he and Cynthia are visiting Derk in the mine, there is a huge collapse and all three are trapped. The only way out is to use dynamite and Roger takes it upon himself to effect an explosion that he knows will cost him his life but will free the other two. After this has been done Cynthia realizes that her husband loves her and that if she proves herself worthy of his love they can have a good life together.

Dynamite does not rate among the great Cecil B. DeMille films, except in the mind of Joel McCrea. "He was very good to me. My part was nothing more than a gloried bit but he built it up and he carried me through the picture. I'm very grateful for that."

THE SILVER HORDE

RKO, 1930;
produced by William Le Baron; directed by George Archainbaud; written by Wallace Smith, based on the novel by Rex Beach; photographed by Leo Tover and John W. Doyle; 76 minutes.

Cast:
Cherry Malotte, Evelyn Brent; *George Balt*, Louis Wolheim; *Boyd Emerson*, Joel McCrea; *Mildred Wayland*, Jean Arthur; *Fraser*, Raymond Hatton; *Queenie*, Blanche Sweet; *Fred Marsh*, Gavin Gordon; *Wayne Wayland*, Purnell Pratt; *Thomas Hilliard*, William Davidson; *Svenson*, Ivan Linow

As if not quite sure how to present the largely unknown Joel McCrea to the public as the leading man of *The Silver Horde*, RKO listed him in both the film's title panel and in all the advertising as "and Joel McCrea," following the names of the principle nine actors in the cast. Evelyn Brent was given top billing, with the powerful but ugly character actor Louis Wolheim taking second. Be that as it may, the plot of *The Silver Horde*, based upon the Rex Beach novel about the salmon industry in Alaska, centers on the character played by McCrea—Boyd Emerson.

After giving up hope of being a gold miner, Emerson, along with his partner Fraser (Raymond Hatton), arrives in the port of Kalvic and finds it a very unfriendly place. The lack of hospitality is due to the town and its salmon cannery business being run by a syndicate headed by Fred Marsh (Gavin Gordon). The only gesture of friendliness comes from Cherry Malotte (Brent), a lady whose name gives pause whenever spoken. It seems she used to run a honky-tonk in Nome. Everybody knows about Cherry - except the innocent young Emerson. She becomes fond of him and suggests he proceed to Seattle, where she can arrange financing to set him up in the salmon business in Kalvic. To look after him she sends her roughneck friend George Balt (Wolheim). Seattle happens to be the city in which Mildred (Jean Arthur), Emerson's bride-to-be, lives. She is a spoiled society girl whose father, Wayne Wayland (Purnell Pratt), is in league with Fred Marsh.

What Emerson does not know is that Cherry, in order to get him a bank loan, has given up her shares in a mining venture. Finding out about this, Wayland and Marsh do all they can to make busi-

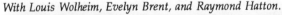

With Louis Wolheim, Evelyn Brent, and Raymond Hatton.

With Jean Arthur.

With Evelyn Brent.

ness as difficult as possible for Emerson. Cherry continues to back him, despite her disappointment in learning that Mildred is the girl he loves. Emerson prospers but reacts with disgust when Marsh tells about Cherry's tawdry past. Emerson tells Cherry he is ashamed to have accepted her help. Mildred, who has now arrived in Kalvic with her father, tells Emerson she is ashamed of his reaction, which plays into Marsh's hands because he wants Mildred for himself. That plan is quashed by Cherry when she arrives at a party and announces that Marsh is still married to her friend, Queenie (Blanche Sweet). Later the angry Balt points out to the confused Emerson that the woman who deserves his love is the faithful Cherry and not the flighty Mildred. Emerson rejects Mildred when she tries to make up with him and goes to Cherry, asking for forgiveness and telling her he loves her.

The critics of 1930 were not much impressed with *The Silver Horde*, pointing out that the Beach novel was so compressed for the 76-minute film that it came off as thin melodrama. They allowed that it did give some good visual accounts of the salmon industry in Alaska (largely beefed up with purchased footage of fishing and cannery activities), but that the relationships between the charac-

ters was old fashioned drivel.

The Silver Horde may not have pleased the critics but it did fairly well at the box office and launched twenty-five-year-old Joel McCrea on a career as a Hollywood leading man. That he seemed at ease in front of the camera is something McCrea attributes to help from Louis Wolheim.

Wolheim, who died of a sudden heart attack in 1931, at the age of fifty-one, started in films in 1919 and won particular attention as the gruff old German soldier who befriends the young Paul Baumer (Lew Ayres) in *All Quiet on the Western Front*, released shortly before *The Silver Horde*. McCrea: "He taught me more in ten weeks than I learned in four years of college. For example, how to keep from looking and feeling self-conscious when you walk into a room. The trick he taught was to look for something in the room that you don't approve of, something you can look at critically. In other words, you deliberately transfer your thinking away from yourself and focus it elsewhere. He used to tell me how mentally lazy I was. 'You've got to think, not act. Your face is expressive enough. When you think, I can read your thoughts. So, if you want to show you are mad, don't scowl, just think mad and you'll look mad.'"

24

LIGHTNIN'

Fox, 1930;
produced and directed by Henry King; written by S.N.
Behrman and Sonya Levien, based on the play by Winchell
Smith and Frank Bacon; photographed by Chester Lyons;
96 minutes.

Cast:
"Lightnin'" Bill Jones, Will Rogers; *Mary Jones,* Louise
Dresser; *John Marvin,* Joel McCrea; *Milly Jones,* Helen
Cohan; *Raymond Thomas,* Jason Robards; *Zeb,* Luke
Cosgrave; *Judge Townsend,* J.M. Kerrigan; *Margaret Davis,*
Ruth Warren; *Mrs. Lower,* Sharon Lynn; *Diana,* Joyce
Compton; *Ronald,* Rex Bell; *Sheriff,* Goodee
Montgomery; *Monte Winslow,* Phillips Tead

With Jason Robards and Will Rogers.

With Will Rogers and Luke Cosgrave.

Will Rogers is so firmly ensconced as an icon of
folksey American humor it is sometimes forgotten
that he was also a major movie star. Following his
years as a cowboy, rodeo entertainer and vaudeville
artist Rogers made the first of his more than sixty
films in 1918. In 1929 he signed with Fox Film
Corporation to make what he called "audiables."
All of his films would be made for that studio at the
rate of three each year. He did them one after the
other in order to get them out of the way and allow
him to travel the world, make radio shows, write
newspaper columns and generally commentate on
the world as he saw it. The fourth of his Fox talkies
was *Lightnin'*, for which he and director Henry
King decided, after considering the possibilities,
that young Joel McCrea would be good for the role
of the lawyer who comes to the aid of the title
character, Lightnin' Bill Jones, and woos his
daughter.

Lightnin' Bill Jones is so called because he moves
with anything but the speed of lightning. He is a
veteran of the Spanish-American War, given to the
telling of tall tales and the imbibing of whiskey, "in
order to ward off possible attacks of malaria." He is
separated from his wife Mary (Louise Dresser),
who owns the Calivada Hotel, which sits astride the
California-Nevada boundary. Its positioning allows
the clientel, mostly wives in pursuit of divorce, to
have a California address while living in the Nevada section of the hotel for the three-month residen-
cy necessary to obtain a divorce in that state. Land
speculators, more aware of the land value than the
owners, try to persuade Mary and her daughter
Millie (Helen Cohan - the daughter of George M.
Cohan in what may have been her only film) to sell.
The signature of Lightin' is needed to do this but
John Marvin (McCrea) advises him against it because he knows the speculators to be crooks. Mar-

vin is living in the California part of the hotel in order to avoid a Nevada summons brought by the very same crooks who have fixed the blame for one of their fraudulanet transactions on him. Mary is persuaded to sue for divorce so that her signature alone can effect the sale but John acts as Lightnin's lawyer and reveals the crooks for what they are. As a consequence Mary takes Lightnin' back into her life and John and Millie fall in love.

The plot of *Lightnin'*, as in any of the Will Rogers pictures, is secondary to his presence. He was hired to be Will Rogers and any scenarist working on the films had to realize that much of what he said came from his mind rather than their scripts. This was a problem for McCrea, who was first introduced to Rogers by Henry King as the two actors were about to shoot a scene in a buggy on location near Lake Tahoe, on the California-Nevada border.

Recalled McCrea, "Our first scene was in the buggy. Will talked quite a bit, then I had a line, and then he talked quite a bit longer. I was waiting for a cue that never came. he stopped and then the director asked me why I didn't continue. I said I didn't hear my cue. Will laughed and said, 'If you're waitin' for cue words this is gonna be a long summer. Fact is, I never do remember lines so good. I get the sense of 'em and trick 'em up a bit.' Then he said, 'Joe,' he always called me Joe, 'Joe, you ain't like these other actors, you're kinda like me, so I'm gonna help you. You see, I change the dialogue, but when I think I've said enough I'll give you a poke and then you talk. I'm not gonna do this for the other actors but I'll do it for you."

Lightnin' was the beginning of a close friendship between Rogers and McCrea. It was a film in which the young actor learned a lot about being natural in front of a camera, or at least appearing to be natural, which remains one of the primary functions of film acting. After the film was shown Rogers let it be known that he wanted to have McCrea in all his films. However, by this time McCrea was under contract to RKO, a studio that kept him busy in their own productions as well as loaning him out to other producers. As it worked out, McCrea would be able to make only one more film with Will Rogers.

ONCE A SINNER

Fox, 1931;
directed by Guthrie McClintic; written by George Middleton;
photographed by Arthur L. Todd; 71 minutes.

Cast:
Diana Barry, Dorothy Mackaill; *Tommy Mason*, Joel McCrea; *Richard Kent*, John Halliday; *Serge Ratoff*, C. Henry Gordon; *Kitty King*, Ilka Chase; *Mrs. Mason*, Clara Blandick; *Mary Nolan*, Myra Hampton; *James Brent*, George Brent; *Hope Patterson*, Sally Blane

If nothing else, *Once a Sinner* established Joel McCrea in the Hollywood scheme of things as a likeable and dependable vis-a-vis for topflight leading ladies. As such he was a type much in demand but in short supply. He was tall, plainly handsome, solidly American; he had a natural sense of ease about him, he spoke well and he did not, a factor of great importance, overwhelm any of the ladies who were clearly the stars of the films in which they appeared.

Here he was teamed with Dorothy Mackaill, the British-born, former Ziegfeld girl who starred in silents all through the Twenties. In *Once a Sinner*, a title which gives away the story, Diana Barry (Mackaill) is that familiar movie figure of bygone days, the lady with a morally shady past. Leaving New York and the company of a rich man who has been keeping her, Diana Barry settles in the small town of Sparta and falls in love with a young inventor, Tommy Mason (McCrea). She tries to tell him

With Sally Blane, George Brent, Dorothy MacKaill, and John Halliday. Myra Hampton has her back to the camera.

about her past but the happy young man is not interested in anything but the present and the future. Soon after they marry he receives an offer which takes he and his new bride to New York.

Complications arise. Richard Kent (John Halliday), who has brought Mason to New York, turns out to be one of those with whom Diana has previously been involved. Intimations of this begin to dawn upon Mason and, terribly jealous, it leads to a separation. Diana meets another old friend, elegant playboy Serge Ratoff (C. Henry Gordon), and she accepts his invitation to go to Paris with he and his fiancee. Ratoff dumps his girl and makes a play for Diana once they are in France. Kent, who is also in Paris, sees the predicament in which Diana is caught and contacts Mason, who is in London on business. Mason angrily goes to Paris, where, after an array of misunderstandings he comes to his senses about the wife who loves him and takes her home.

The romantic and comedic fluff of *Once a Sinner* was a depth-of-Depression audience pleaser, as were most films of that era which dealt with the romantic problems of the wealthy, especially those in which the leading ladies wore a variety of attractive dresses. For McCrea it proved that he could appear in such films and not look ridiculous, or as the critic of *The New York Times* put it, "Mr. McCrea rises to what is demanded of him in his part."

KEPT HUSBANDS

RKO, 1931;
produced by William Le Baron; directed by Lloyd Bacon; written by William Sarecky, Forrest Halsey and Alfred Jackson; photographed by Jack MacKenzie; 76 minutes.

Cast:
Dot, Dorothy Mackaill; *Dick,* Joel McCrea; *Parker,* Robert McWade; *Mrs. Parker,* Florence Roberts; *Mrs. Post,* Clara Kimball Young; *Mrs. Brunton,* Mary Carr; *Gwen,* Lita Chevret; *Hughie,* Ned Sparks; *Bates,* Bryant Washburn; *Mr. Post,* Freeman Wood

RKO had loaned Joel McCrea to Fox for *Once a Sinner* and sensing that it would do well at the box office they borrowed Dorothy Mackaill from First National to again match her with McCrea in one of their own vehicles. To make the title of *Kept Husbands* even more enticing it was advertised with the slogan, "Every Inch a Man - Bought Body and Soul by His Wife." Once again Mackaill plays a lady of some means, but this time McCrea is a lad of poor background.

Dick Brunton (McCrea) is an ambitious young man who works in a steel mill. One day he rescues three workers from a burning pit and his employer (Robert McWade) offers him a reward of a thousand dollars, which Brunton proudly refuses. He does,

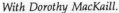
With Dorothy MacKaill.

however, accept an invitation to be a dinner guest at his employer's mansion where he meets the spoiled daughter, Dot Parker (Mackaill). Dinner table talk reveals that Brunton was a star football player while in college. After dinner, Dot boasts to a friend that she will land Brunton in a month, which she does. Accustomed to getting what she wants, she manoeuvres him into marriage.

Following a lavish honeymoon through Europe, the pair settle down to a lifestyle in keeping with the bride's background but at odds with his much more modest upbringing. Brunton finds himself elevated to managerial rank at the steel mill. He spends his days in his office studying projects on paper rather than at the structural level he would prefer, and in the evenings he takes his bride to concerts and society functions. Whenever he professes his frustrations she smothers him with affection.

Finally he explodes in anger, and as he leaves the house, she reminds him of the part her father's wealth has played in his success. The anger subsides as she realizes that she really loves her husband and that she must compromise in order to get him back. They reconcile when he gets the kind of work he really wants at the mill, at a salary he believes he can rightfully earn, and when Dot agrees to live within that income.

The moral of *Kept Husbands* is all too obvious, that poor men who marry rich women face the loss of their self respect. McCrea struggled with the part as best he could, although it required little beyond looking sullen for much of the time. It was easier for Dorothy Mackaill, playing the frivolous and spoiled bride, traipsing around in furs and gowns. *Kept Husbands* did only fair business; after a half dozen more programmers like this one Mackaill decided to retire from the movies. She was thirty-two when she did so in 1934.

With Constance Bennett.

BORN TO LOVE

RKO, 1931;
directed by Paul L. Stein; written by Ernest Pascal;
photographed by John Mescall; 84 minutes.

Cast:
Doris Kendall, Constance Bennett; *Barry Craig*, Joel McCrea; *Sir Wilfred Drake*, Paul Cavanagh; *Lord Ponsonby*, Frederick Kerr; *Leslie Darrow*, Anthony Bushell; *Lady Ponsonby*, Louise Closser Hale; *Duchess*, Mary Forbes; *Evelyn Kent*, Elizabeth Forrester; *Tom Kent*, Edmund Breon; *Fop*, Reginald Sharland; *Tibbetts*, Daisy Belmore

Although she began her film career in the Twenties and continued into the Fifties, Constance Bennett was essentially a Hollywood star of the Thirties. One of the three daughters of Broadway matinee idol Richard Bennett, her feisty screen image was abetted by a private life of considerable color. On screen she was mostly a lady of gumption overcoming any adversity her scenarists could invent, be she a hard-done-by shopgirl or a high society playgirl. No matter the level of society Constance handled it all with style and humor - and a large wardrobe.

In 1931, Bennett found herself at RKO when the studio to whom she was under contract (Pathe) merged with RKO. The studio operated for two years under the banner RKO-Pathe. During this time she appeared in eight films.

Doris Kendall (Bennett) is an American nurse serving in a British military hospital. In London she meets Barry Craig (McCrea), a US Army pilot and they fall in love. They try to marry but an army regulation forbids an officer to have a wife in the war theatre in which he is serving. This does not stop them from becoming lovers in the few remaining days before he is sent to France. A few months later Doris is informed that Craig has been shot down behind German lines and is presumed dead. The sadness is made worse by the fact she is pregnant with Craig's child. She confides this to a kindly British army officer, Sir Wilfred Drake (Paul Cavanagh) who has long been in love with her. She accepts his proposal of marriage and settles into an aristocratic English life.

A year later Craig, only wounded in action and hospitalized, returns to London to find the girl he loves. When Doris learns of his survival she must see Craig. Sir Wilfred cannot accept this and forces her to make a choice. She chooses Craig, which results in the loss of custody of her child. More sadness follows when the child dies of a sudden illness. However, Doris is now in the arms of the man she loves, and who loves her.

Born to Love did well with the market to which it was aimed despite all the critical comment about it being a maudlin tearjerker. The pairing of McCrea with Constance Bennett was potent enough for RKO to line up another vehicle immediately.

THE COMMON LAW

RKO, 1931;
produced by Charles R. Rogers; directed by Paul L. Stein; *written by John Farrow and Horrace Jackson, based on the novel by Robert W. Chambers; photographed by Hal Mohr; music direction: Arthur Lange; 77 minutes.*

Cast:
Valerie West, Constance Bennett; *John Neville, Jr.,* Joel McCrea; *Cardemon,* Lew Cody; *Sam,* Robert Williams; *Clare Collis,* Hedda Hopper; *Stephanie Brown,* Marion Shilling; *Querido,* Paul Ellis; *John Neville, Sr.,* Walter Walker

The Common Law, released in the summer of 1931, shamelessly exploited the Constance Bennett image of 'tarnished lady' on the screen and lively lady of the tabloids. The film was emblazoned with an advertising banner reeking with implied sophisticated immorality: "Noted for her Beauty... Notorious for her Indiscretion. She didn't care what people said as long as one lone man kept saying 'I Love You.' Her beauty made him the world's greatest artist. But in gaining a reputation for him, she lost her own!"

For Joel McCrea it was a first fling at playing a scion of high society. John Neville, Jr. (McCrea), is an American painter living amid Left Bank bohemians in Paris on family funds . Valerie West (Bennett) is an American girl who has become bored with being the live-in inamorata of an arrogant Frenchman, Cardemon (Lew Cody), and offers herself to Neville as a model. He needs a beautiful girl as the model for a nude nymph he is painting. Their working relationship blossoms into romance but

With Constance Bennett.

abates when he learns of her sordid past. They part but Neville finds his lust overcoming his moral precepts; when they meet again at a lavish Parisian artists' ball they fall into each other's arms and decide to live together in a common law marriage.

When Neville's high society sister, Clare (Hedda Hopper), hears about this scandalous situation she gets Neville to return to their Tarrytown, New York, mansion on the pretext that their father (Walter Walker) is gravely ill. Young Neville shocks his sister by turning up with Valerie. Clare schemes to reveal Valerie's past by staging a party aboard the family yacht, to which she invites the notorious playboy Cardemon. Clare's plans to have her brother marry someone in their own set is partly sabotaged by the fact that their father thinks Valerie is wonderful, which helps junior come to his senses and make her his legitimate wife. Junior has a fistfight with Cardemon, and after a few harsh words about the quality of his society friends he and Valerie leave the boat to find happiness elsewhere.

The improbable plotlines of *The Common Law* meant little to 1931 film audiences who made the film a winner for RKO. The plot was secondary to seeing the elegant, cheeky Constance Bennett doing her stuff as a modern-thinking young lady winning her love by thumbing her nose at old society conventions. To her leading man McCrea, it was a definite step up the career ladder.

GIRLS ABOUT TOWN

Paramount, 1931;
directed by George Cukor; written by Raymond Griffith and Brian Marlow, based on a story by Zoe Akins; photographed by Ernest Haller; 66 minutes.

Cast:
Wanda Howard, Kay Francis; *Jim Baker*, Joel McCrea; *Marie Bailey*, Lilyan Tashman; *Benjamin Thomas*, Eugene Pallette; *Jerry Chafe*, Alan Dinehart; *Mrs. Thomas*, Lucille Webster Gleason; *Alex Howard*, Anderson Lawler; *Edna*, Lucille Brown; *Webster*, George Barbier; *Simms*, Robert McWade; *Hattie*, Louise Beavers

For the last of the five films in which he appeared in 1931, RKO sent Joel McCrea to Paramount to play opposite Kay Francis, one of the sultriest leading ladies of the period. McCrea probably felt at home on the set because the job was much the same sort of work that he had been doing at RKO - playing the morally upright young man amid the company of not so morally upright young ladies. In the case

of *Girls About Town* the girls are of the kind who hire out for goodly sums of money as companions to out—of—town business men. The screenplay is based on a treatment that Zoe Akins had made of her 1930 play *The Greeks Had a Word for It*, albeit a word that could not be used in a 1931 Hollywood movie. One of the earliest films directed by George Cukor, it presents its girls as gold diggers, but the kind who say "Good night" at the door when brought home.

The two main girls are the lively Wanda (Francis) and the soulful Marie (Lilyan Tashman), who share a plush apartment and often date in tandem. They meet a pair of business men from Michigan, quiet, withdrawn Jim Baker (McCrea) and rotund, blustery Benjamin Thomas (Eugene Pallette), when they are invited to attend a party on a yacht. While swimming Jim rescues Wanda from drowning. They begin to fall in love even though Jim has made plain his distaste for ladies of loose values. Their affair goes astray when Jim discovers that Wanda is married, although she is separtated from her husband. The husband Alex (Anderson Lawler) turns up and threatens to blackmail Jim, who immedi-

With Kay Francis.

ately backs off after hearing about Wanda's questionable lifestyle. Wanda decides to put up a fight in order to win him and in the process finds that her marriage has been legally invalid for some time. With this, and her protestations of love and reformation, she manages to melt Jim's heart.

Girls About Town stands up as a slick piece of movie entertainment, much to the credit of Cukor's sense of style. For film historians it is an interesting example of how Hollywood artfully played around with the censorial restrictions of 1931. Part of that art involved presenting the hero in films of this type as being almost puritanical in his bearing, and in view of his five films that year Joel McCrea would seem to have been the personification of American Morality.

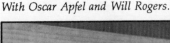

BUSINESS AND PLEASURE

Fox, 1932;
produced by A.L. Rockett; directed by David Butler; written by William M. Conselman and Gene Towne, based on the

novel The Plutocrat by Booth Tarkington and the play derived from it by Arthur F. Goodrich; photographed by Ernest Palmer; 77 minutes.

Cast:
Earl Tinker, Will Rogers; *Madame Momora*, Jetta Goudal; *Lawrence Ogle*, Joel McCrea; *Mrs. Tinker*, Dorothy Patterson; *Olivia Tinker*, Peggy Ross; *Arthur Jones*, Cyril Ring; *Ben Wackstle*, Jed Prouty; *Hadj Ali*, Mitchell Lewis; *Sheik*, Boris Karloff; *P.D. Weatheright*, Oscar Apfel; *Charles Turner*, Vernon Dent

A little less than a year after making *Lightnin'*, Joel McCrea got his wish to work again with Will Rogers when RKO loaned him to Fox for *Business and Pleasure*. Unfortunately, neither this nor *Lightnin'* would be remembered as being among the great humorist's best movies. The best of the Rogers movies are *A Connecticut Yankee* (1931), *State Fair* (1933), *David Harum* (1934), *Judge Friest* (1934) and *Steamboat Round the Bend* (1935).

In *Business and Pleasure* Rogers plays an Oklahoma razor-blade manufacturer named Earl Tinker. He takes off for Syria to try to buy the secrets of Damascus Steel. With him, and pretending to be tourists on what is a business venture, are his wife

With Oscar Apfel and Will Rogers.

With Peggy Ross.

(Dorothy Peterson) and his daughter Olivia (Peggy Ross). On the ocean liner crossing the Atlantic, Olivia meets young playright Lawrence Ogle (McCrea) and the two fall in love. A mysterious lady passenger known as Madame Momora (Jetta Goudal) makes a play for Earl. She is doing it as an assignment from a rival razor-blade manufacturer. Her job is to discover his plans and foil them.

Madame Momora charms the Tinker family as she introduces them to Syrian life but her machinations lead Earl closer to death than to finding out how Damascus Steel operates. He finds himself caught between two warring Arabian tribes and narrowly escapes execution when captured by one of them by adopting the disguise of an ancient, bearded mystic and faking a radio broadcast. He exposes the devious Madame Momora to the Arab leader (Boris Karloff) and brings about an end to the war, which leads to a contract with Damascus Steel.

McCrea's role in *Business and Pleasure* was both less appealing and less important than the one in *Lightnin'*, and RKO was not pleased with the results. They were building him as a leading man, and this was not the kind of material in which they wished him to appear. This was apparent even when they loaned him to Fox for the film. Their contract stipulated that "the name of Joel McCrea not be preceded in the billing by the names of more than two other members of the cast, in type as large as that used for any other member of the cast, except Will Rogers." Be that as it may, the business dealings between the studios and the fact that Mc-Crea was never to appear in another Rogers film made no difference to the friendship between the two men. McCrea saw plenty of Rogers in the remaining four years of the great humorist's life.

THE LOST SQUADRON

RKO, 1932;
produced by Louis Sarecky; directed by George Archainbaud; written by Wallace Smith, Herman Mankiewicz and Robert Presnell, based on a story by Dick Grace; photographed by Eddie Cronjager; music by Max Steiner; 79 minutes.

Cast:
Captain Gibson, Richard Dix; *Follette Marsh*, Mary Astor; *Von Furst*, Erich von Stroheim; *The Pest*, Dorothy Jordan; *Red*, Joel McCrea; *Woody*, Robert Armstrong; *Fritz*, Hugh Herbert; *Detective*, Ralph Ince

With Richard Dix.

After a pair of Fox loan-outs that they felt did not do Joel McCrea a great deal of good, RKO decided to give him an heroic role in a major production, *The Lost Squadron*, a film about Hollywood. Based on a story by stunt pilot Dick Grace, who also appears in the film as an aviator, the plot deals with a group of ex-World War I pilots now working in movies about the war they have just fought. RKO spiked the ads with some blazing lines: "Batteries of cameras swung aloft against the skies where America's aces streak, plunge, soar, dive, crash at the command of a madman!" The madman in this case is a sadistic director named Von Furst, played to the hilt by Erich Von Stroheim, Hollywood's foremost purveyor of Germanic sadism and madness in the years between the first and second World Wars.

A trio of out-of-work pilots, Gibson (Richard Dix), Red (McCrea) and Woody (Robert Armstrong), arrive in Hollywood having heard there is employment for flyers in the movies. They are assigned to a film about the war being directed by Von Furst, and since they are required to be American fighter pilots attacking German bombers the job

seems to be nothing more than a non-lethal, better paid version of what they were doing previously. What they had not counted on is the spiteful, heartless nature of the director, who thinks nothing of risking lives to get realistic effects - or of being murderously vengeful.

Prior to the war Gibson was in love with Follette Marsh (Mary Astor) but he returned to find her the wife of Von Furst. Sensing that some affection lingers between Gibson and his wife, Von Furst plans to do away with the flyer during the course of a film stunt. He pours acid on the wing struts of Gibson's bi-plane but Red and Woody discover the corrosion. Woody, who has been enjoying a life of carousing and drinking, decides to take the plane up himself because Gibson had once saved his life. Red finds out about this too late to stop him but he tells Gibson, who takes up another plane in an attempt to stop Woody from doing the stunt, but to no avail. Woody plunges to his death.

Red seizes Von Furst before Woody takes off, ties him up and swears to kill him if Woody dies. Confined to a hangar, Von Furst breaks out during a storm and is shot by Red as he tries to run away. Red hides the body. Woody's sister, known as the Pest (Dorothy Jordan), who is in love with Red, prevents the investigating detective (Ralph Ince) from finding the body. In the meantime, Gibson carries the body to his plane, takes the plane aloft and then deliberately crashes it, costing him his life. Gibson, it seems, has also been in love the The Pest, but he knew she would be happier with Red, who now cannot be blamed for killing the vicious director.

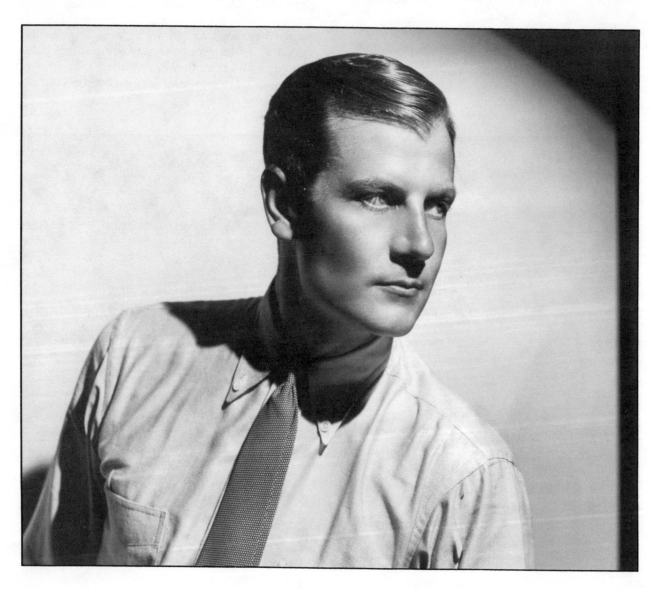

The melodramatics of *The Lost Squadron* border on the absurd but the film offers good footage in its aviation sequences and provides yet one more attempt by Hollywood to present itself as being even more wicked than it really is. For Erich von Stroheim it was a juicy role, so absurd as to be ripely enjoyable. For Joel McCrea it was a solid part as a romantic hero, carried off with sufficient panache to give RKO greater confidence in his marketability.

BIRD OF PARADISE

RKO, 1932;
produced by David O. Selznick; directed by King Vidor; written by Wells Root, Leonard Praskins and Wanda Tuchok; photographed by Clyde De Vinna, Edward Cronjager and Lucien Androt; music by Max Steiner; 80 minutes.

Cast:
Luana, Dolores Del Rio; *Johnny,* Joel McCrea; *Mac,* John Halliday; *Chester,* Richard "Skeets" Gallagher; *Thornton,* Lon Chaney, Jr.; *Hector,* Bert Roach; *The King,* Napoleon Pukui; *Mahumahu,* Sofia Ortega

With Dolores Del Rio and Napoleon Pukui.

When twenty-nine year old David O. Selznick took over as Head of Production at the financially desperate RKO Radio Pictures in November of 1931, he inherited a number of story properties from his predecessor, William Le Baron. One of them was Richard Walton Tully's stage play *Bird of Paradise.* Selznick thought the best way to film the story was to make it as lush and grand as possible, and to that end sent a copy of the play to King Vidor, whose direction of such films as *The Big Parade* (1925), *The Crowd* (1928) and *The Champ* (1931), had given him high esteem in the industry. Vidor replied that he found the material so dull that he could not finish reading it, to which Selznick admitted that he had not read it either but that he instinctively felt it could be made into a juicy picture. "I want Del Rio and McCrea in a South Seas Romance. Just give me three wonderful love scenes like you had in *The Big Parade* and *Bardelys the Magnificent.* I don't care what story you use so long as we call it *Bird of Paradise* and Del Rio jumps into a flaming volcano at the finish."

With leeway such as this Vidor decided to take on the assignment, agreeing with Selznick that the best thing would be to go to a genuine tropical paradise to film it. In January of 1932, Vidor and his chief writer, Wells Root, left San Francisco for the five-day voyage to Hawaii thinking they would whip the script into shape in that time. It turned out to be a terribly rough crossing, during which no writing was done. They had a week in Hawaii to finish the script before the cast and crew arrived. On the second day of shooting it started to rain. Vidor: "It was the worst onslaught that the islands had experienced in twenty years. If the skies cleared even for a few hours, we would gather together our hundred extras and rush out with all our equipment. Then, as if we had engendered the rain God's wrath, the heavens would darken, the winds would come again, and the downpour defy us in attempts to make progress."

After thirty-five days on location, Vidor and his company returned to California - with only about half of what they needed to complete the film. Back in Hollywood Selznick made arrangements for further beach shots to be filmed on Catalina Island; for a native village to be built on the backlot; and for the underwater sequences to be shot in the water tank at the Warner-First National Studios in Burbank. Despite the strained budget, Selznick hired Busby Berkeley to choreograph the native dances, and he asked Max Steiner to write as sumptuous a music score as possible. Steiner more than met the

With Dolores Del Rio.

challenge; *Bird of Paradise* became the first film to have a music score from beginning to end, nonstop. The film was finally completed in June of 1932, making it one of the longest in-production movies to that time.

The plot of *Bird of Paradise* is simple. It begins with the arrival of an American yacht in Tahiti. Happy natives swim out to meet the Americans. That evening the guests are entertained by the natives with a feast and dance but the fun is spoiled by a medicine man who objects to the interest Johnny (McCrea) and Luana (Del Rio), the daughter of the King, are taking in each other. The following morning Luana swims out to the yacht and Johnny joins her in a playful swim, after which he chases her onto the shore and introduces her to the art of kissing. When the yacht leaves Tahiti, it leaves without Johnny.

The lovers' idyll is shattered by the medicine man and his party. They beat Luana, take her away and leave Johnny tied to a tree. He is later released by a sympathetic native woman. Luana is instructed by her father to marry a native prince but Johnny interupts the wedding and whisks Luana away. The two swim to another island.

When a volcano erupts on the main island, the natives, thinking that the gods are angry because of what Luana has done, come for her and leave Johnny unconscious. He attempts to rescue her as she is prepared as a sacrifice to placate the gods, but he is

wounded and thrown into the same hut with her. The next day, as the natives lead both Luana and Johnny off to the volcano, his friends with the yacht return and rescue the pair. That evening Luana bids goodbye to the sleeping Johnny and swims back to join her people, believing it is her duty to save them from godly wrath. In ceremonial attire she sacrifices herself in fiery death for the peace of the island.

Bird of Paradise did well with the public but it was never able to recoup its $800,000 expense. As a result, Selznick dropped his plans for *Green Mansions* another lush, tropical McCrea-Del Rio romance. McCrea was seen for the first time as a truly romantic leading man, wearing swimming trunks instead of drawing-room suits. In fact, never again would McCrea appear in material as sexual or as exotic as in *Bird of Paradise*. His scenes with the beautiful Dolores Del Rio have genuine passion about them, especially as he lies next to her in the bushes and teaches her about kissing; and, the underwater flirtation scenes caused quite some comment in 1932. Del Rio, or her double as she later claimed, appears to be nude, although frame enlargements make it apparent that the lady is wearing brief, skin-colored shorts. With McCrea in white trunks the flirtation in the water is indeed sensual, but as was always the case with anything dircted by King Vidor, the eroticism was tasteful.

McCrea, almost desperate at the time to appear in something more exciting than the rather dreary

With "Skeets" Gallagher, John Halliday (with gun), and Bert Roach.

romances to which he had been assigned, claims that the film came his way while he was giving surfboard lessons to David O. Selznick at the Santa Monica beach. Selznick promised him the part if McCrea succeeded in teaching him how to surf. The Head of Production never learned to surf, but he cast McCrea anyway, saying to him, "I always keep my word."

THE MOST DANGEROUS GAME

RKO, 1932;
produced by Merian C. Cooper and Ernest B. Schoedsack; directed by Ernest B. Schoedsack and Irving Pichel; written by James Creelman, based on a story by Richard Connell; photographed by Henry Gerrard; music by Max Steiner; 78 minutes.

Cast:
Bob Rainsford, Joel McCrea; *Eve Trowbridge,* Fay Wray; *Zaroff,* Leslie Banks; *Martin,* Robert Armstrong; *Ivan,* Noble Johnson; *Tartar,* Steve Clemento; *Captain,* William Davidson

A small luxury schooner makes its way at night through the passageway between the mainland and an island in the tropics. The worried captain explains to the owner that the navigational lights in the channel do not conform to the markings on his chart. The owner is enjoying a party with his guests and, tells him not to worry. A moment later the ship hits a reef and slips beneath the dark, shark-infested waters. There is only one survivor, an American hunter-author named Robert Rainsford, who swims to the island and collapses on the beach. He awakes to find himself in a rocky, thickly forested area, through which he makes his way to a huge fortress-like building. He knocks on the door and becomes the guest of a tuxedo-attired Cossack nobleman, a refugee of the Russian revolution who calls himself Count Zaroff.

With Fay Wray.

With Leslie Banks.

Thus the opening of *The Most Dangerous Game*, a taut, compact little film that has acquired a minor cult following for its stylish sets and almost-horror suspense. Producer Merian C. Cooper had long had the idea of filming Richard Connell's novelette about a hunter who becaomes the hunted, and once RKO gave him permission to proceed with his *King Kong*, Cooper set up production on his *The Most Dangerous Game*, devising ways of utilizing the same jungle sets as well as two members of the *King Kong* cast, Fay Wray and Robert Armstrong. It also allowed composer Max Steiner to write what is practically a prelude to his celebrated score for the big ape.

Coming right after his success with *Bird of Pardise*, the part of Robert Rainsford was a boon for Joel McCrea, giving him heroic scope as the hunter who outwits the wiley Zaroff, played with overly ripe dramatics by English actor Leslie Banks. For Fay Wray, it was also something of a prelude since her role as fellow captive Eve Trowbridge required her, as did the role of Ann Darrow in *King Kong*, to run around the jungle in a dress that becomes increasingly tattered and revealing.

The core of the story is that the elegant and seemingly hospitable Count Zaroff is a hunter who believes that the greatest of all hunts is that which involves hunting his fellow man. He has caused previous ship wrecks and after entertaining his guests he advises them that their only chance to escape is to accept his challenge of taking to the jungle with a head start. Thus it is with Robert Rainsford, whom Zaroff regards as his greatest challenge since he has read Rainsfords' books on hunting and greatly respects him. Rainsford's doubt about Zaroff are confirmed when he and Eve discover the count's cellar museum in which the Count has preserved the heads of his previous victims, which include Eve's brother Martin (Armstrong). It now becomes a battle of wits between Rainsford, equipped with only a knife, and Zaroff, with his bow and arrow. Eve decides to go with Rainsford, hoping that they will find the one boat on the island by which they can escape.

Zaroff advises Rainsford that if he can elude capture for a full day he will be a free man, but adds, "To date, I have not lost."

With that Rainsford and Eve take off into the dense jungle, with its foggy swamps and rocky cliffs. Rainsford eludes the crafty Zaroff, who finally resorts to bringing on his pack of vicious hounds. Cornered on a rocky ledge, Rainsford kills one dog but falls into the sea when he tackles another. Zaroff takes Eve back to the house but his celebration is spoiled by the arrival of Rainsford, who explains how he survived the fall. Zaroff appears to accept

39

defeat but in handing over the keys to the boathouse he also pulls a pistol, fires and misses. In the ensuing fight Rainsford manages to stab Zaroff in the back with one of his own arrows. After Rainsford and Eve escape to the boat, they look back to see Zaroff fall from his high window into the yard filled with his hounds.

The Most Dangerous Game remains a neat little film. RKO re-made it in 1946 as *A Game of Death*, with John Loder in the McCrea role, and again as *Run for the Sun* (1956), with Richard Widmark as the hunted hunter. Neither film has quite the ambiance of the 1932 original, which was released in England as *The Hounds of Zaroff*. The Merian C. Cooper version, made in collaboration with his *King Kong* partner Ernest R. Schoedsack, has much the same atmosphere as their classic *King Kong*.

Simpler to make than the elaborate *King Kong*, *The Most Dangerous Game* was released several months earlier, and for students of *King Kong* the settings are interesting to spot. The swamp through which McCrea and Wray trudge is exactly the same as the one in *King Kong*. The stretch of jungle through which Zaroff runs in pursuit of his quarry is the same as that through which a sailor in *King Kong* is chased by a dinosaur. Both sequences were filmed on the same day. The set in which Kong shakes his terrified pursuers off a log over a chasm was used the next day for the scene in which McCrea and Wray cross the log in eluding Zaroff.

Direction for *The Most Dangerous Game* is credited to both Schoedsack and Irving Pichel, with the former handling the jungle sequences and Pichel directing the interior material. And with so much of its costs being covered by *King Kong*, *The Most Dangerous Game* was produced on a budget of $150,000, remarkable by even 1932 standards.

THE SPORT PARADE

RKO, 1932;
directed by Dudley Moore; written by Corey Ford, Tom Wenning and Francis Cockerell, based on a story by Jerry Horwin; photographed by J. Roy Hunt; 63 minutes.

Cast:
Sandy Baker, Joel McCrea; *Johnny Brown*, William Gargan; *Irene*, Marian Marsh; *Morrison*, Walter Catlett; *Dizzy*, Richard "Skeets" Gallagher; *Radio Commentator*, Robert Benchley

In an obvious attempt to broaden Joel McCrea's he-man image, RKO next placed him in a movie which required him to portray a professional athlete who is adept at every sport he tackles. College sports films were once almost as numerous as musicals; usually they dealt with the hero who overcomes personal problems to shine on the campus football field. This one is a little different in that it begins in college and then follows the hero as he tries to make a living out of the reputation garnered in school.

As *The Sport Parade* begins, Dartmouth is playing Harvard and Dartmouth's wonder boys, Sandy Baker (McCrea), and Johnny Brown (William Gargan) lead the team to victory, as they always have. The Baker-to-Brown pass has become legendary in the Halls of Ivy. After graduation the sensible Brown turns down offers to become a pro athlete, opting instead to become a newspaper sports writer. However, the fun-loving Baker is persuaded by Morrison (Walter Catlett), a slick promoter to give professional football a fling. He finds pro football a lot tougher and much less sentimental than the the college game, and things begin to go badly for him.

Brown's girlfriend Irene (Marian Marsh), who has always had a soft spot for Baker, helps to bring him together with his former school chum and Bak-

With Marian Marsh.

er joins the paper to write a column in tandem with Brown. Things go well for a while but Baker's heart is not in journalism. Again he succumbs to the wiley Morrison, who persuades Baker to take up wrestling, where easy money can be made by those who know how to handle themselves in what is clearly more a phoney stunt racket than a sport.

The unsavory nature of his new "sport" becomes apparent to Baker when Morrison asks him to fake a defeat, to "take a dive." Baker's reluctance is backed up by Irene, who asks him to do the honorable thing and at least try to win. Baker does exactly that, and in winning the fight also wins Irene. Brown, who has long realized he has been losing his girl to his old friend, gives his blessing.

Trimmed to a brief 63 minutes, *The Sport Parade* is closer to a B picture than an A, and none too convincing, especially in its final sequence in which McCrea beats a hefty pro wrestler. Of interest is an array of 1932 sports events, but the film gives the impression that the sports industry was as full of sharks then as it is now.

ROCKABYE

RKO, 1932;
produced by David O. Selznick; directed by George Cukor; written by Jane Murfin, based on the play by Lucia Bronder; photographed by George D. Ellis; music by Max Steiner; 75 minutes.

Cast:
Judy Carroll, Constance Bennett; *Jacobs Van Riker Pell,* Joel McCrea; *Anthony de Sola,* Paul Lukas; *Snooks Carroll,* Jobyna Howland; *Al Howard,* Walter Pidgeon; *Brida,* Clara Blandick; *Jimmy Dunn,* Walter Catlett; *Mrs. Van Riker Pell,* Virginia Hammond; *Fagin,* J.M. Kerrigan; *Lilybet,* June Filmer; *District Attorney,* Charles Middleton

George Cukor, justly celebrated for his skill in wringing great performances from famous actresses, was not pleased at being assigned to direct *Rockabye.* However, like its two stars, Constance Bennett and Joel McCrea, he was under contract to

With Paul Lukas and Constance Bennett.

RKO and expected to do as he was told, especially under the command of the forceful young David O. Selznick. The studio had bought the rights to the stage play and even though Selznick admitted the material was claptrap, RKO was not about to waste their investment. Cukor had just scored hits with *Bill of Divorcement* and *What Price Hollywood?*, and if anybody could make the material work, he could. Selznick further hedged his bets by assigning Bennett, the star of *What Price Hollywood?* Joel McCrea was dragged in halfway through the production of *Rockabye* to replace Philips Holmes. Selznick became displeased with Holmes' performance and ordered all of Bennett's scenes with him re-shot with McCrea.

The film opens with a sensational trial in New York, where stage star Judy Carroll (Bennet) has been called in as a character witness for indicted politician Al Howard (Walter Pidgeon), with inferences that they were lovers having a good time on public money. Howard is exonerated but the unsavory press coverage causes Judy to lose the child she had adopted. The agency condemns her milieu as unfitting for the decent upbringing of a child.

To escape her sorrows she takes off for a giddy tour of Europe. She brings back with her a new American play she has found in Paris, *Rockabye* by Jacobs Van Riker Pell. She askes her devoted manager, Anthony de Sola (Paul Lukas), to locate the author, even though he feels the story about a prostitute who gives up her child is not suitable for her image. Pell (McCrea), a product of high society, visits her and agrees with the manager that she is not right for the part. But the clever and alluring actess soon changes his mind and in no time at all the two of them are madly in love with each other. Separated from his wife, Pell asks Judy to marry him once he is divorced and she happily agrees.

The play opens with great success but the author is not at the opening. Judy's puzzlement at his absence is soon cleared by a visit from Mrs. Van Riker Pell (Virginia Hammond), Jacob's elegant mother, who explains that her son has just become a father and that, even though separated, his duty is now with his wife and child. Pell comes to see Judy and he tells her he still loves her but admits confusion. "What's the right thing to do?" he asks. She tells him he had better go back to his family, backing up the advice with the fib that she is in love with her manager. The melancholy Pell leaves and as he does the manager turns to Judy and tells her, "You're a great lady."

Constance Bennett's flamboyand playing of the cheeky actress hiding a heart of gold gives *Rockabye*

what little credibility is can muster. Her leading man deserves credit for having been able to get through the whole silly business without choking on his lines.

THE SILVER CORD

RKO, 1933;
produced by Pandro S. Berman; directed by John Cromwell; written by Jane Murfin, based on the play by Sidney Howard; photographed by Charles Rosher; music by Max Steiner; 74 minutes.

Cast:
Christina Phelps, Irene Dunne; *David Phelps*, Joel McCrea; *Hester*, Frances Dee; *Robert Phelps*, Eric Linden; *Mrs. Phelps*, Laura Hope Crews; *Delia*, Helen Cromwell

The cord of the title is very much umbilical and the silver is more than a little tarnished. Sidney Howard's play *The Silver Cord* was a virtual indictment of American mother love and the film softened the impact not at all. Laura Hope Crews, possibly best remembered as the dithery Aunt Pittypat in *Gone With the Wind* (1939), starred in the play on Broadway and was wisely used by RKO for their cinema version. Although she received fifth billing, Crews is really the star of the vehicle, with the other four main characters mostly reacting to her. The characterization is that of a wealthy widow who has endured an unhappy marriage and clings to her two sons, the strong David Phelps (McCrea) and the weak Robert (Eric Linden), with a possessiveness bordering on ownership.

The film opens in Heidelberg where the brilliant young research biologist Christina Phelps (Irene Dunne), newly married to David, agrees to return to New York so that he may accept a position as an architect. Before taking the post, David takes his wife home for a first meeting with his mother at their palatial country home. There Christina meets her brother-in-law Robert and his lovely bride-to-be, Hester (Frances Dee). Mrs. Phelps wastes no time in telling Christina that there is a difference in womanly virtues between their generations, that modern women like Christina seem more interested in careers than in being dutiful wives. Later she tells David the "No woman can love a man the way a mother does," following it with a plea not to go to New York but to stay in the area where she can help him set up business.

42

With Frances Dee, Laura Hope Crews, and Irene Dunne.

David is much less affected by his mother's sly campaign to control him than is Robert, whom she convinces is too good for Hester. She tells him not to make the mistake David has made. The distraught Hester leaves the house in the middle of a winter night and flings herself in a break in a frozen river. David spots her, runs after her and saves her. The doctor who attends Hester advises Robert that his mother is not the physically weak woman she pretends to be, indeed it would take a stick of dynamite to kill her, but this does not release him from her domination.

Hoping to get at David, Mrs. Phelps pleads that Robert is close to a nervous breakdown and that she has not the strength to cope with it alone. David vacillates. Christina does not. She tells Mrs. Phelps that her love is abnormal and that when she herself becomes a mother she hopes her love for her children will not be romantic and possessive. Christina gives David his choice — his wife or his mother. He hesitates and she leaves, taking Hester with her. David deliberates for only a moment before running after his wife and joining her in the taxi she has ordered, and the woeful Robert stays with his mother.

RKO first considered Katherine Hepburn and then Ann Harding for the part of Christina. Finally it went to Irene Dunne, who had scored a hit the previous year with *Back Street* and was clearly a star in ascendency. Dunne's own strength of character, matched with humor and style, was perfect for Christina, the kind of woman who would indeed offer a man a straight choice between herself and his mother.

With Joel McCrea, she got a leading man who would clearly make the right choice. His role of the upright, cheerful David waffles only in those scenes in which he gives serious thought to staying close to the family home in order to support his mother. His strong image makes the scenes less than convincing and all McCrea can do with them is register confusion. There is nothing, however, confusing about Laura Hope Crews' limning of the seemingly gentle but actually tough Mrs. Phelps. She had scored a hit with the Theatre Guild's production of the Pulitzer Prize winning play and the film is hers at every turn.

For McCrea *The Silver Cord* is a film for which he has fond memories - not because of the material but because it brought him together with the delightful Frances Dee, whose performance as the rejected Hester is one of the film's strengths. She and McCrea began a courtship that led to their marriage a few months later.

SCARLET RIVER

RKO, 1933;
produced by David Lewis; directed by Otto Browser; written by Harold Shumate; photographed by Nicholas Musuraca; 57 minutes.

Cast:
Tom Baxter, Tom Keene; *Judy Blake,* Dorothy Wilson; *Jeff Todd,* Creighton Chaney (Lon Chaney, Jr.); *Babe Jewell,* Betty Furness; *Ulysses Mope,* Roscoe Ates; *Sam Gilroy,* Edgar Kennedy; *Buck Blake,* Billy Butts; *Clink McPherson,* Hooper Atcheley; *Benny,* Jack Raymond; *Dummy,* James Mason; *Yak,* Yakima Canutt; *with guest stars* Joel McCrea, Myrna Loy, Julie Hayden *and* Bruce Cabot.

After *The Silver Cord,* Joel McCrea made a brief appearance in RKO's excellent little western *Scarlet River,* which starred Tom Keene as a Hollywood cowboy. A spoof on the making of westerns, Keene portrays a cowboy star making a movie on location, during the course of which he tackles a band of real outlaws. Before going out on location he is seen walking to the studio commissary just as McCrea is walking out. The two enter into some brief banter and McCrea kids Keene about the hazards of being a movie hero. Keene then goes into the commissary where he says hello to the likes of Myrna Loy and Bruce Cabot. The fact that RKO used their stars as guests shows that *Scarlet River* would likely turn out to be a cut above the standard B western. It most certainly is.

BED OF ROSES

RKO, 1933;
produced by Merian C. Cooper; directed by Gregory La Cava; written by Wanda Tuchok and Eugene Thackrey; photographed by Charles Rosher; music by Max Steiner; 67 minutes.

Cast:
Lorry Evans, Constance Bennett; *Dan Walters,* Joel McCrea; *Minnie,* Pert Kelton; *Father Doran,* Samuel S. Hinds; *Steve Paige,* John Halliday

Joel McCrea was teamed with Constance Bennett for the fourth and final time in *Bed of Roses,* a film that was greeted by the critics with faint praise. RKO billed it as the story of a girl who "took a short-cut down the primrose path to make herself a bed of roses." In other words, it was another of Bennett's portrayals of tough, cheeky ladies who thumb their noses at society but who usually end

With George Reed and Constance Bennett.

up choosing true love. Years later, when a writer asked her to comment on her films for a career profile, Bennett asked, "Did I really make a film called *Bed of Roses*?"

This is the story of Lorry Evans (Bennett) who, in company with her pal Minnie (Pert Kelton), is released from a reformatory and opts for a life of ease, mostly achieved by fleecing men. The two girls take a boat down the Mississippi and are caught trying to rob passengers. When the Captain comes to grill Lorry she jumps overboard and is picked up by Dan Walters (McCrea), who owns a cotton barge.

The generous young man is smitten with Lorry and despite her amorous feelings for him she is determined to get to New Orleans to live the good life. She steals money from Dan and takes off.

In New Orleans, she meets and woos gentlemanly book publisher Steve Paige (John Halliday), but she cannot get good, honest Dan Walters out of her mind. When she talks of returning to him, the jealous Paige tells her he will expose her shabby past to Dan. This does not keep her from leaving Paige, and taking a job as a clerk in a department store, where Dan eventually finds her. Lorry confes-

45

ses her past and he comforts her by saying that it does not matter, he loves her and wants her and their barge home is waiting.

Constance Bennett made only one more film for RKO before she began free lancing. Sensing that the kind of material she had been given by RKO was fast becoming passe, Bennett wisely decided on different kinds of vehicles, scoring a hit with *Topper* in 1937. For Joel McCrea, the Bennett pictures had at least given him wide exposure. In the case of *Bed of Roses* it also brought him into contact with Gregory La Cava, a director McCrea rates very highly. "He was great with actors. He took people like me, when I really didn't know very much, and he treated me with ease. He had absolute confidence in himself, in what you could do and in what he could tell you to do. And you did it."

ONE MAN'S JOURNEY

RKO, 1933;
produced by Pandro S. Berman; directed by John Robertson; written by Lester Cohen and Samuel Ornitz, based on the story Failure by Katharine Havilland-Taylor; photographed by Jack MacKenzie; 72 minutes.

Cast:
Eli Watt, Lionel Barrymore; *Sarah*, May Robson; *Letty McGinnis*, Dorothy Jordan; *Jimmy Watt*, Joel McCrea; *Joan Stockton*, Frances Dee; *McGinnis*, David Landau; *Bill Radford*, James Bush; *Jimmy Watt (age 6)*, Buster Phelps; *John Radford*, Oscar Apfel; *May Radford*, June Filmer

RKO next gave Joel McCrea a role in a serious vehicle, albeit one in which he was definately not the star. *One Man's Journey* is one man's film - Lionel Barrymore, borrowed from MGM to play the part of a dedicated doctor of the old "general practisioner" kind.

Eli Watt (Barrymore) is a man who after the death of his wife returns to the rural community from which he came, having found little success in big city medicine. He now decides to devote himself to his own people, administering to their needs even though it sometimes brings no fee other than food from his farmer patients. Eli also serves as a healer of social troubles as well as affairs of the heart. He helps his ward Letty (Dorothy Jordan), whom he had reared since he brought her into the world at the cost of her mother's life. His biggest concern is his son Jimmy (Buster Phelps as the boy and McCrea as the adult), guiding him on his cho-

With Frances Dee.

sen career as a doctor. Eli also comes to his son's aid in courting a girl (Frances Dee) from a family not sympathetic to the match.

In this tale of self-sacrifice and noble dedication, the old doctor finally gets recognition from his colleagues when he is honored at a medical gathering. However, his real satisfaction comes from knowing that his son is now a very successful doctor and happily married.

The film is Lionel Barrymore's all the way, tracing the career of the doctor over a thirty year period. A few years later Barrymore would shine playing the crusty old Dr. Gillespie in the Dr. Kildare series at MGM, but in *One Man's Journey* he is a paragon of kindly understanding, and convincingly so. For McCrea it was a relatively easy assignment, and a relief from some of the fluff in which he had been appearing. The film did well with the public and five years later RKO made it again, under the title *A Man to Remember*, with Edward Ellis as the old doctor and Lee Bowman in the McCrea role.

CHANCE AT HEAVEN

RKO, 1933;
produced by Merian C. Cooper; directed by William Seiter;
written by Julian Josephson and Sarah Y. Mason, based on
the story by Vina Delmar; photographed by Nick Musuraca;
music by Max Steiner; 70 minutes.

Cast:
Marje Harris, Ginger Rogers; *Blacky Gorman*, Joel
McCrea; *Al*, Andy Devine; *Glory Franklyn*, Marion
Nixon; *Mrs. Franklyn*, Virginia Hammond; *Mr. Harris*,
Lucien Littlefield; *Mrs. Harris*, Ann Shoemaker; *Sid
Larrick*, George Meeker; *Betty*, Betty Furness; *Chauffeur*,
Herman Bing

Joel McCrea had little reason to be pleased about
his next assignment which required him to play
opposite twenty-two year old Ginger Rogers in another flimsy romantic drama. Rogers had by this
time appeared in a dozen or so movies but had yet
to make much of an impression with the public.
Chance at Heaven was completed before *Flying Down
to Rio*, Rogers first teaming with Fred Astaire, but
RKO wisely released it after the *Flying Down to Rio*
opening at the Radio City Music Hall in late Decem-
ber of 1933. It may have helped a little, the Astaire-
Rogers impact being as strong as it was, but nothing
short of a screening in heaven could have saved this
film.

In *Chance at Heaven*, McCrea is Blacky Gorman, a
car mechanic and the owner of a gas station in a
small town. Blacky's relationship with his sweet-
heart Marje (Rogers) goes off the track when
wealthy society girl Glory Franklin (Marion Nixon)
drives her powerful roadster into his station and
takes a shine to him. The ambitious Blacky is soon
seduced by the glamorous life, which leads to his
marriage to Glory. Glory's no-nonsense mother

With Ginger Rogers and Marian Nixon.

(Virginia Hammond) disapproves of the marriage and does all she can to make it a failure. Blacky finds that being married to the light headed Glory is much less than he thought it might be. So he heads back to Elm Corners, where the faithful and understanding Marje takes him back, and where he will presumably lead the kind of life he was meant to lead. *Chance at Heaven* is a film neither Joel McCrea nor Ginger Rogers recalls with any fondness.

GAMBLING LADY

Warner Bros, 1934;
produced by Henry Blanke; directed by Archie Mayo; written by Doris Malloy and Ralph Block; photographed by George Barnes; 66 minutes.

Cast:
Lady Lee, Barbara Stanwyck; *Garry Madison*, Joel McCrea; *Charlie Lang*, Pat O'Brien; *Peter Madison*, C. Aubrey Smith; *Sheila Aiken*, Claire Dodd; *Steve*, Philip Reed; *Don*, Philip Faversham; *Mike Lee*, Robert Barrat; *Fallin*, Arthur Vinton; *Cornelius*, Ferninand Gottschalk; *Graves*, Robert Elliott; *Pryor*, Arthur Treacher

Barbara Stanwyck already had a dozen film roles under her belt by 1934. Following a few years as a dancer and actress in New York, she began her Hollywood career in 1929, at the age of twenty-two. She quickly established herself as a reliable player who seemed to personify the modern American woman - self-assured, down-to-earth, a little flippant and very appealing. That image came across clearly in *Gambling Lady*, where she played a female gambler named Lady Lee, an instinctive but always honest gambler.

For reasons that he cannot recall, Joel McCrea was loaned by RKO to Warner Bros., probably in one of those player swapping deals that was normal between the studios in those years. Whatever the reason, it turned out well for McCrea because it brought his first contact with Stanwyck. The two became friends and would boost each other's career, appearing together in six more films after this one.

Early in the film Lady's father, Mike (Robert Barrat) commits suicide after being caught up in the meshes of a big gambling syndicate headed by Fallin (Arthur Vinton). Her friend Charlie Lang (Pat O'Brien) helps her financially but she turns him down when he proposes marriage. She goes to work for the syndicate as a card dealer and meets

With Barbara Stanwyck.

socialite gambler Garry Madison (McCrea). He falls in love with her and she does not discourage him. He mistakenly involves her in a card game with two policemen, which leads to her arrest. She believes Madison has turned her in and turns down his offer to bail her out of jail. Later, after Charlie has bailed her out, she learns that Madison had nothing to do with the arrest and she marries him.

Trouble arises when Sheila Aiken (Claire Dodd) makes a play for Madison while he and Lady are in Monte Carlo, where Lady's skills almost break the bank. Back in America, it is Lady's turn to bail out Charlie, using money gained by pawning jewelry Lady had won from Sheila in a game. Someone murders Charlie and Madison is arrested as a suspect. He is released when Lady finds that Madison was with Sheila at the time of the murder. To exact this information Lady promises Sheila that she will divorce Madison. The divorce is granted, against the wishes of Madison's crusty old father (C. Aubrey Smith) who is fond of his daughter-in-law. Madison senior now does some sleuthing that proves Sheila was responsible for Charlie's death hoping to cover up her own nefarious involvement in gambling. Lady and Madison are brought happily together.

Gambling Lady is a typical Warner Bros. crime picture of its time, a kind the studio had almost patented—a brisk 66-minutes, taut, slick and glib. It served Stanwyck better than McCrea, who regarded it as simply another loan-out. That attitude was apparent to Stanwyck, who brough him to task about it. McCrea: "The first day, just before noon, they started taking stills and the Warner publicity people didn't seem to be interested in me. They were taking shots of Barbara and Pat O'Brien and C. Aubrey Smith, and when they didn't call me I went off for lunch. I expected a blast from the director, Archie Mayo, when I got back, but instead I got it from Stanwyck, 'Where the hell were you for the stills?' I tried to say I wasn't very important to Warners and she said, 'Listen, kid, if you want to make it in this business, be professional. You come to work like you would if you were digging postholes on a ranch. If you want to get ahead, get your ass in there and do what you're supposed to do.' I was a little hurt by this but I had brains enough to realize she was absolutely right. I did what she said and by the end of the picture we were great friends."

HALF A SINNER

Universal, 1934;
directed by Kurt Neumann; written by Earle Snell and Clarence Marks, based on the play Alias the Deacon by John B. Hymer and LeRoy Clemens; photographed by George Robinson; 70 minutes.

Cast:
Phyllis, Sally Blane; *John Adams*, Joel McCrea; *Deacon*, Berton Churchill; *Mrs. Clarke*, Alexandria Carlisle; *Louella*, Gay Seabrook; *Willie*, Mickey Rooney; *Jim Cunningham*, Spencer Charters; *Slim Sullivan*, Russell Hopton; *Bull Moran*, Guinn Williams

RKO next loaned him to Universal for what was virtually a role in support of character actor Berton Churchill. Based on the play *Alias the Deacon*, in which Churchill had starred on Broadway, about a genial card shark who poses as a Deacon. As played by Churchill, one of Hollywood's most employed character players right up until his death in 1940 at age sixty-four, the Deacon is a lovable rascal who cheats only those who can afford it and who acts as a benefactor for those in need.

A kind of minor league Elmer Gantry, the Deacon travels by freight train between the towns he affably assaults. On one of these box car trips he meets a young couple down on their luck, John Adams (McCrea) and his girl Phyllis (Sally Blane). The couple settle in Harrington, Kansas, where John gets a job as a garage mechanic and Phyllis as a hotel cashier. When the Deacon turns up in town, they are afraid he might expose them as box car drifters but he instead befriends them in his holy guise - as he goes about his high handed business of giving moral uplift at church meetings and indulging in no-limit poker games behind the barber shop. When John is arrested on suspicion of robbery, it is the Deacon who discovers the real culprits.

First filmed in 1927 with Jean Hersholt as the Deacon, Universal made it for the third time in 1940, with hillbilly comic Bob Burns in the lead and Dennis O'Keefe playing the McCrea role. Both the 1927 and 1940 versions used the original title, *Alias the Deacon*, which might have served better in 1934 than the feeble *Half a Sinner*. McCrea was far from pleased with this loan-out, especially when he read the New York Times review which noted that "The young lovers fall into the most tedious of patterns and are not worth the space the film devotes to them."

With Sally Blane.

THE RICHEST GIRL IN THE WORLD

RKO, 1934;
produced by Pandro S. Berman; directed by William A. Seiter; written by Norman Krasna; photographed by Nick Musuraca; music by Max Steiner; 80 minutes.

Cast:
Dorothy Hunter, Miriam Hopkins; *Tony Travers,* Joel McCrea; *John,* Henry Stephenson; *Sylvia,* Fay Wray; *Philip,* Reginald Denny; *Donald,* George Meeker; *Preston,* Burr McIntosh; *Butler,* Edgar Norton; *Orsatti,* Wade Boteler

Miriam Hopkins, like Constance Bennett, was a star of the Thirties; and like Bennett, she specialized in ladies who suffered at the hands of men, whether she's playing a floozie or a society belle. She was a better actress than Bennett, although she lacked Bennett's sense of humor. Her stock was high in 1934. A star of the stage in the Twenties, Hopkins had made her first film in 1931, *Fast and Loose.* She won critical and public approval as Ivy, the doomed barmaid in *Dr. Jekyll and Mr. Hyde* (1932) opposite Fredric March, with whom the following year she also appeared in the Ernst Lubitsch romantic comedy *Design for Living.* In 1934 she signed a contract with Samuel Goldwyn and was immediately loaned to RKO for *The Richest Girl in the World,* a thinly disguised account of super wealthy Barbara Hutton.

The film needed a handsome young leading man and RKO lost no time in casting Joel McCrea. RKO advertised the picture with the slogan "the season's most electrifying comedy drama, lavish with humor, romance and glamour," and even allowing for hyperbole the claim was slightly nearer the truth than usual. The script was an original screenplay by Norman Krasna, then beginning a distinguished Hollywood career, and his witty dialogue and appealing characters were fully backed by RKO with stylish sets and a great deal of attractive costuming. Such costuming was a vital audience factor in 1934.

The story line is simple. Dorothy Hunter (Hopkins), long tired of being romanced because of her money and deeply suspicious of men while at the same time much in need of genuine love, decides on a ruse: she travels incognito with her married friend Sylvia (Fay Wray) and swaps identity with her. Sylvia poses as Dorothy and Dorothy pretends to be the secretary of the world's richest girl. Among the men she meets is Tony Travis (McCrea).

He charms her but in order to find out the mettle of his character she keeps inventing ways of pushing him into the arms of Sylvia. Eventually she decides that Travis is the man for her.

The Richest Girl in the World was a winner for RKO, for Miriam Hopkins, as well as for McCrea, although in a way that he could not at first have expected. By now he had decided to leave RKO; he had not liked some of the films to which they had assigned him, nor was he happy with the loan-outs, but he felt he now had enough of a reputation as a reliable and popular leading man to be able to more personally direct the course of his career. Marion Hopkins played an important part in his next decision. She liked McCrea and felt he was exactly the kind of actor with whom she could function, one of little emotion who would not conflict with her own very emotional style. She was largely responsible for getting McCrea a contract with Samuel Goldwyn, and she would appear with McCrea in four Goldwyn films.

With Miriam Hopkins.

PRIVATE WORLDS

Paramount, 1935;
Produced by Walter Wanger; Directed by Gregory La
Cava; Written by Lynn Starling, based on the novel by
Phyllis Bottome; Photographed by Leon Shamroy;
84 minutes.

Cast:
Dr. Jane Everest, Claudette Colbert; *Dr. Charles Monet*,
Charles Boyer; *Sally MacGregor*, Joan Bennett; *Dr. Alex
MacGregor*, Joel McCrea; *Claire Monet*, Helen Vinson;
Matron, Esther Dale; *Dr. Arnold*, Samuel Hinds; *Carrie*,
Jean Rouverol; *Tom Hirst*, Sam Godfrey; *Bertha Hirst*,
Dora Clement; *Dr. Harding*, Theodore von Eltz; *Dr.
Barnes*, Stanley Andrews; *Jerry*, Guinn 'Big Boy'
Williams.

With Joan Bennett.

Once Joel McCrea left RKO in 1934, he never
returned to that studio. He could not complain of
exposure for he had appeared in twenty films in
only five years, but he was not content with the
quality of most of them, especially the loan-outs. He
felt he could do better guiding his own career, a
brave stand for even a well established name to
take in 1934. In the years to come McCrea would
sign contracts with studios, but they would not be
for long terms and they would not be exclusive. His
first offer after leaving RKO was the Paramount
production *Private Worlds*, where he received fourth
billing and in which he appeared only because director Gregory La Cava insisted on him playing the
part. Producer Walter Wanger wanted Robert Montgomery, with Douglas Fairbanks, Jr. as second
choice. La Cava, who had used McCrea in *Bed of
Roses*, had his way. When Wanger pointed out that
McCrea was not as good an actor as either Montgomery or Fairbanks, La Cava replied, "He will be
with me."

Private Worlds was the first major Hollywood
film to deal with clinical psychiatry, an unusually
serious subject with which to win movie audiences
in the mid-Thirties. Wanger hedged his bets by
starring the popular Claudette Colbert and the
darkly romantic French actor Charles Boyer. Set for
the most part in a sanatorium, albeit one seemingly
as comfortable as a country club, the plot lines deal
with several lives - doctors as well as patients. Doctors Jane Everest (Colbert) and Alex MacGregor
(McCrea) are dedicated to curing the mentally ill by
enlightened modern methods. The ambitious Mac-
Gregor is bitterly disappointed in his quest for the
superintendent's post when French doctor Charles
Monet (Boyer) is brought in to take the post. Dr.
Jane sympathizes with MacGregor but feels her

duty is to the institution and its patients, which
means taking whatever assignments given her by
Monet.

To assuage his frustrated ambitions, MacGregor
takes up with Monet's sister Claire (Helen Vinson),
to the consternation of MacGregor's wife Sally
(Joan Bennett). Following an experience with an
insane girl (Jean Rouverol), Sally's mind cracks and
she is injured in a fall. Together Jane and Monet
perform an operation that saves Sally's life. Upon
hearing that his sister is directly responsible for the
situation Monet orders her from his home. The near
tragedy brings MacGregor to his senses and he now
decides to pay more attention to his loving wife,
and a little less to his work. Monet, learning that
Jane intends to leave the hospital, goes to her to
plead with her to stay, not only as his associate but
as his wife.

Private Worlds, an almost forgotten film, stands
up well with its fine scripting, acting and direction,
giving an intelligent accounting of the psychiatric
methods of its time. The public reaction was good
although the studio clearly tilted it in the direction
of female rather than male customers. However,
one male who held the film in high regard was
McCrea, mostly because of the director. "He was
great with actors. He took me when I really didn't
know too much and treated me with ease. He had
absolute confidence in himself and he made me feel
confident. He knew what you could do and you did
it, and it didn't matter how many takes or how
much time it took. The producer had to wait - we
were making a picture. He was a very good writer

and he worked on the scripts of his films. He knew if lines were right, just as he knew which actors he wanted."

OUR LITTLE GIRL

Fox, 1935;
Produced by Edward Butcher; Directed by John Robertson; Written by Stephen Avery, Allen Rivkin and Jack Yellin, based on the story *Heaven's Gate* by Florence Leighton Pfalzgraf; Photographed by John Seitz; Music by Oscar Bradley; 63 minutes.

Cast:
Molly Middleton, Shirley Temple; *Elsa Middleton,* Rosemary Ames; *Dr. Donald Middleton,* Joel McCrea; *Rolfe Brent,* Lyle Talbot; *Sarah Boynton,* Erin O'Brien-Moore; *Clown,* Poodles Hanneford; *Amy,* Margaret Armstrong; *Alice,* Rita Owen; *Jackson,* Leonard Carey; *Mr. Tramp,* J. Farrell MacDonald.

Shirley Temple celebrated her seventh birthday while working on *Our Little Girl* for Fox, the studio that had now had her under contract for more than a year. Starting in short films at the age of four, this incredible child - the only one in film history who could do everything, be it acting, singing or dancing - had appeared in small roles for other studios before Fox wisely locked her in. In 1934 she became box office gold, starring in *Bright Eyes* and *The Little Colonel*. Then came *Our Little Girl* and Joel McCrea's chance to play opposite the Mighty Moppet. However, it is not a movie either Temple or McCrea could regard as being high on their list of triumphs.

The story is simple. Dr. Donald Middleton (McCrea) is very successful and ambitious with his medical research and spends very little time at home with his wife Elsa (Rosemary Ames) and their happy daughter Molly (Temple). He makes the mistake of allowing a friendly neighbor, wealthy play-boy Rolfe Brent (Lyle Talbot), to take Elsa to various social functions in his stead. What starts out innocently enough becomes serious as Rolfe falls in love with Elsa, abetted by Elsa's mistaken notion that her husband's devoted nurse Sarah Boynton (Erin O'Brien-Moore) is a rival. Sarah would be if she could, but Middleton has no interest in her at all. Gradually little Molly finds herself the victim of a divided family, with talk of mother marrying Brent. Feeling that she is not wanted she decides to leave home.

With Shirley Temple and Poodles Hanneford.

With Rosemary Ames and Shirley Temple.

With Rosemary Ames and Shirley Temple.

Walking along a lane, Molly comes across a kindly tramp (J. Farrell MacDonald), to whom she confides her troubles. Middleton has alerted the police of his missing child but he finds Molly with the tramp, who gives him some advice about love and family. With this, Molly and her parents reunite and Sarah Boyton and Rolfe Brent realize they do not stand a chance with the Middletons.

Our Little Girl pleased the Temple fans, who ignored the critical view that it was mere fluff. However, memories of this film were soon eclipsed by a roster of Temple successes that included *Curly Top*, *The Littlest Rebel* and *Captain January*, one after the other. In her autobiography Shirley Temple recalls *Our Little Girl* as a production in which she tried to romance Joel McCrea, who called her Butch, but that he was usually occupied with reading the script. At one point she asked him, "Is it true you're married to someone else?" He replied, "Yes, but you're still my special friend." So ended the Temple-McCrea affair.

WOMAN WANTED

MGM, 1935;
Produced by Phil Goldstone; Directed by George B. Seitz; Written by Leonard Fields and Dave Silverstein, based on a story by Wilson Collison; Photographed by Charles Clarke; Music by William Axt; 68 minutes.

Cast:
Ann, Maureen O'Sullivan; *Tony Baxter*, Joel McCrea; *District Attorney*, Lewis Stone; *Smiley*, Louis Calhern; *Sweeney*, Edgar Kennedy; *Betty*, Adrienne Ames; *Peedles*, Robert Greig; *Joe Mertz*, Noel Madison; *Casey*, Granville Bates; *Collins*, William B. Davidson; *Lee*, Richard Powell.

Joel McCrea's next call was from MGM, to play opposite the winsome Maureen O'Sullivan, who had by this time already established herself as Tarzan's Jane and had turned up in just about every MGM version of costumed romance derived from Great Literature. Her refined manner and British diction made her perfect for that kind of role but less so for something like *Woman Wanted*, in which she was a murder suspect in a contemporary American setting. McCrea is the battling lawyer who loves and saves her.

The film has an interesting opening scene. Law-

With Maureen O'Sullivan.

BARBARY COAST

United Artists, 1935;
Produced by Samuel Goldwyn; Directed by Howard Hawks; Written by Ben Hecht and Charles MacArthur; Photographed by Ray June; Music by Alfred Newman; 97 minutes.

Cast:
Mary 'Swan' Rutledge, Miriam Hopkins; *Louis Chamalis*, Edward G. Robinson; *Jim Carmichael*, Joel McCrea; *Old Atrocity*, Walter Brennan; *Col. Marcus Aurelia Webb*, Frank Craven; *Knuckles Jacoby*, Brian Donlevy; *Oakie*, Clyde Cook; *Jed Slocum*, Harry Carey; *Peebles*, Otto Hoffman; *Joseph Wigham*, Rollo Lloyd; *Sawbuck McTavish*, Donald Meek; *Sandy Ferguson*, Roger Gray; *Judge Harper*, J.M. Kerrigan.

After placing Miriam Hopkins under contract, Samuel Goldwyn announced many ambitious projects for her. However, in four years with him she wound up in only four Goldwyn films, all of which starred her opposite Joel McCrea. The astute producer, however, not only made money with those pictures but also profited handsomely by loaning her to other producers. Her first Goldwyn film, *Barbary Coast*, took a long time to reach completion. Wanting to make a spectacular film about early California, Goldwyn bought Herbert Asbury's novel *Barbary Coast*, but found it was largely a chronicle of crimes on the San Francisco waterfront. Undeterred he instructed his scenarists, the estimable

With Edward G. Robinson and Miriam Hopkins.

yer Tony Baxter (McCrea) carries on an across-the-traffic-lights flirtation with Ann (O'Sullivan). She is sitting in a police car, having just left court where she has been convicted of a murder charge rigged by gangsters because they think she has secret information dangerous to their safety. Gangster chief Smiley (Louis Calhern), causes an accident by driving his car into the police vehicle. In the ensuing confusion Ann jumps out and gets into Baxter's car. Later she explains her predicament to him and he offers to help her. He gradually falls in love with her as they are harried by both the police and the gangsters. Finally, they are trapped by both groups, and a shoot-out ensues in which Smiley is mortally wounded. Smiley then confesses that he is the perpetrator of all the crimes, including the framing of Ann.

Woman Wanted is typical program product of the mid-Thirties, disigned for double bills and playable as either the top or the bottom feature. MGM's expertise with this kind of picture made it superior to the B pictures turned out by most of the other studios, especially when they featured such talent as Lewis Stone and Louis Calhern. McCrea was getting tired of doing this sort of thing and felt his career needed a boost. He was about to get it.

With Miriam Hopkins.

Ben Hecht and Charles MacArthur, to write a completely original screenplay while retaining the title of the novel. Filming began in the Spring of 1934, with Gary Cooper in the lead and William Wyler directing. Goldwyn disliked the way the project was going and cancelled it. He assigned Cooper to another film, told the writers to come up with another concept, then borrowed Edward G. Robinson from Warner Bros., and hired Howard Hawks to direct. Now satisfied that he had the elements he wanted, *Barbary Coast* went into production.

Despite the tough, dark setting of violence and crime, the central character of the story is a girl, Mary Rutledge (Hopkins), who arrives in San Francisco to get married but finds her intended husband has been killed. She ignores the advice of newspaper publisher Marcus Aurelius Cobb (Frank Craven) to return to her refined New England home and instead takes a job as a hostess in the Bella Donna gambling palace, which is owned by the notorious Louis Chamalis (Robinson). She brings a measure of peace to the rowdy operation by persuading Cobb to quit writing about its unsavory clientele, knowing that if he does not, it will cost him his life.

While making a trip through the gold fields, Mary meets young prospector Jim Carmichael (McCrea), who assumes she is a member of San Francisco's high society. He is disillusioned when he sees her operating the roulette wheel in the Bella Donna. Carmichael gets drunk and loses heavily.

The hard heart of Chamalis is softened by Mary but he will not tolerate any other man's interest in her. Finding out about Carmichael, who he suspects is in love with Mary, Chamalis orders him killed. That plan is sidetracked when the vigilantes, formed to bring law and order to the area, close in on Chamalis and his operation following the murder of Cobb. With many of his men eliminated, the furious Chamalis decides to kill Carmichael himself. The young man is wounded but to save his life Mary offers to return to Chamalis. He has a change of heart and decides to let the lovers go their way while he turns to battle the vigilantes, a battle he knows will end his life.

Barbary Coast was an audience pleaser and the critics praised its production values and the dominate presence of Edward G. Robinson. Hopkins received good notices as the noble heroine and McCrea was mentioned as a serviceable leading man. However, the film proved to be much more than that for him. Miriam Hopkins had been helpful in getting him the part, and once he began filming Goldwyn decided that McCrea was someone he would like to have under contract. It was a major step forward for McCrea, putting him into the prestigious Goldwyn stable and increasing his Hollywood standing considerably.

SPLENDOR

United Artists, 1935;
Produced by Samuel Goldwyn; Directed by Elliott
Nugent; Written by Rachel Crothers; Photographed by
Gregg Toland; Music by Alfred Newman; 77 minutes.

Cast:
Phyllis Manning Lorrimore, Miriam Hopkins; *Brighton
Lorrimore,* Joel McCrea; *Martin Deering,* Paul Cavanagh;
Mrs. Lorrimore, Helen Westley; *Clarrissa,* Billie Burke;
Martha Lorrimore, Katharine Alexander; *Edith Gilbert,*
Ruth Weston; *Clancy Lorrimore,* David Niven; *Major
Ballinger,* Arthur Treacher; *Fletcher,* Ivan F. Simpson;
Baron von Hoffstatter, Torben Meyer; *Billy Grimes,*
Reginald Sheffield.

Within days of finishing *Barbary Coast,* Joel Mc-
Crea and Miriam Hopkins were assigned to *Splen-*

With Arthur Treacher and Miriam Hopkins.

dor, a vehicle far more typical of Samuel Goldwyn
than his foray into rough California history. Despite
his own modest origins, Goldwyn was a man with a
taste for elegance and gravitated to stories about
American high society. This lead him to this story
by Rachel Crothers that she had attempted and
failed to develop into a play. Goldwyn liked it
enough to hire her to develop it into a film.
Crothers' *Splendor* has a satiric bite to it. The story is
about a Park Avenue family, the Lorrimores, who
have run out of money but not social pretensions.

Brighton Lorrimore (McCrea) marries a nice
county girl, Phyllis (Hopkins), and brings her home
where his haughty mother (Helen Westley), his social butterfly sister (Katherine Alexander), and his
wastrel brother (David Niven) all make it obvious
that they disapprove. They were hoping Brighton
would marry a wealthy society girl and bring the
family some much needed affluence. Brighton suggests they sell the family residence and move into
something more modest. His mother has other ideas, most of which center upon breaking up his
marriage. When her nephew, wealthy industrialist
Martin Deering (Paul Cavanagh) comes to visit and
takes a fancy to Phyllis, mother promotes the flirtation, especially since Deering is in a position to set
Brighton up in business, one that will likely call for
a good deal of traveling.

Brighton falls into the trap. While he is away,
Phyllis spends a lot of time with Deering at various
social gatherings in the belief it is helping her husband's career. Gradually it dawns upon her she is
being used and she pleads with Brighton to give up
the job. He does not agree and after further misunderstandings she decides to leave him. Phyllis takes
a job and starts divorce proceeedings, which bring
Brighton to his senses. He turns on his family, ejects
them from the house in which he is the sole owner
and advises them all to look for work. Now, having
been convinced by Phyllis that he should be a writer, he gets a job as a newspaper reporter. In turn,
she tells him that his idea of starting their married
life afresh in an aprartment sounds like "splendor."

Splendor was less than its grand title might have
implied, but it amused the customers in 1935, and it
led Goldwyn to announce the next McCrea-
Hopkins picture would be *Navy Born.* That, as did
so many of his announced projects for Hopkins,
proved to be false. However, he clearly intended to
pair the actor and the actress again. They worked
well as a team, and as the critic for *The New York
Times* noted, "Mr. McCrea and Miss Hopkins are
excellent in their roles."

56

THESE THREE

United Artists, 1936;
Produced by Samuel Goldwyn; Directed by William
Wyler; Written by Lillian Hellman, based on her play;
Photographed by Gregg Toland; Music by Alfred
Newman; 93 minutes.

Cast:
Martha Dobie, Miriam Hopkins; *Karen Wright*, Merle
Oberon; *Dr. Joseph Cardin*, Joel McCrea; *Mrs. Lily Mortar*,
Catherine Doucet; *Mrs. Tilford*, Alma Kruger; *Mary
Tilford*, Bonita Granville; *Rosalie Wells*, Marcia Mae
Jones; *Evelyn*, Carmencita Johnson; *Joyce Walton*, Mary
Ann Durkin; *Agathe*, Margaret Hamilton; *Helen Burton*,
Mary Louise Cooper.

Lillian Hellman's 1934 stage play *The Children's
Hour* dealt with lesbianism, which by the censorial
standards of the time made it an impossible vehicle
for transference to the screen... except in the sly
mind of Samuel Goldwyn. In acquiring the rights,
he knew he would create a controversy, and that he
would have to change not only the thematic subs-
tance but the title. This might have seemed daunting to any producer other than Goldwyn, who both
solved his problem and created even more attention
by hiring Hellman to write the screenplay.

In the play the lives of two school teachers are
almost ruined by malicious gossip about their
implied relationship. In the film Hellman created a
similar problem by having the teachers in love with
the same man, with a gossip implying clandestine
arrangements. Thus *These Three*, a trio made miser-
able by lies and nasty innuendoes.

Goldwyn felt he was doing well with the teaming of Joel McCrea and Miriam Hopkins and that
they would be perfect for the Hellman picture.
Along with Hopkins, he had been cultivating Merle
Oberon as an exotic screen beauty. He shrewdly
cast her as the ladylike Karen Wright, who, in partnership with the rather chilly Martha Doie (Hopkins), opens a private school for girls in New
England. Karen is in love with Dr. Joseph Cardin
(McCrea) and he with her, but Martha also loves
him, although she keeps these feelings to herself.

One of their students, Mary Tilford (Bonita
Grandville), senses Martha's anguish and starts a
rumor that the teacher and the doctor made love in
a bedroom adjacent to the girls' dormitory. The
vicious Mary, a compulsive liar, blackmails another
student, Rosalie (Marci Mae Jones), into backing her
story by threatening to expose her theft of a watch.
The rumor sets off a chain reaction of scandalous
accusations that eventually result in parents with-
drawing their children from the school.

The doctor and the teachers complain to Mary's
grandmother (Alma Kruger), who happens to be
one of the most powerful figures in the community,

With Alma Kruger, Merle Oberon, and Miriam Hopkins.

With Merle Oberon.

film did not match the power and the poignancy of the other.

TWO IN A CROWD

Universal, 1936;
Produced by Charles R. Rogers; Directed by Alfred E. Green; Written by Lewis R. Foster, Dorris Malloy and Earle Snell; Photographed by Joseph Valentine; Music by Herman Heller; 82 minutes.

Cast:
Julia Wayne, Joan Bennett; *Larry Stevens*, Joel McCrea; *Toscani*, Henry Armetta; *Lille Eckklebeger*, Allison Skipworth; *Flynn*, Nat Pendleton; *James Stewart Anthony*, Reginald Denny; *Jonesy*, Andy Clyde; *Skeeter*, Elisha Cook, Jr.; *Bennett*, Donald Meek; *Tony Bonelli*, Bradley Page; *The Lawson Girl*, Barbara Rogers; *Purdy*, John Hamilton; *Charles Brooke*, Tyler Brock; *Ralston*, Douglas Wood; *Kennedy*, Milburn Stone.

but the grandmother believes Mary's claims. This makes the situation even more searing for the trio. In time, Karen begins to suspect that there is something between Martha and the doctor, which causes Martha to confess to Karen her unrequited love.

When Karen tells the doctor she is no longer interested, he decides to go to Vienna. Martha, realizes that she can never win the doctor and makes the decision to leave the school after forcing a confession from Mary, exonerating the three people she has maligned. The contrite grandmother now becomes an ally by relaying a message from Martha to Karen that the doctor is in Vienna and that it would be wise to go to him.

Of the films McCrea made for Goldwyn, *These Three* is by far the best. It is a true classic thanks to the fine script by Hellman, the firm direction of William Wyler, the superb photography of the masterly Gregg Toland, and the sensitive score of Alfred Newman. Bonita Granville was nominated for an Academy Award in the first year of the Supporting Actress category, but she lost to Gale Sondergaard for *Anthony Adverse*.

In 1962, Wyler remade the film, using the play's original title, with Audrey Hepburn and Shirley McClaine as Karen and Martha, and James Garner as the doctor. He also returned to the original subject matter, the implication of lesbianism. Ironically, Wyler's *The Children's Hour* was not nearly as successful as his *These Three*. A subject that had been prohibitive in the Hollywood of 1936 raised few eyebrows twenty-six later. Beyond that, the new

Any actor under contract to Samuel Goldwyn could expect to be loaned out to other studios since he produced a small number of films annually and a considerable part of his income was generated from loaning talent. Joel McCrea's first loan-out under Goldwyn was to Universal for *Two in a Crowd*, which required him to play opposite Joan Bennett in a mild comedy about the horse racing business.

The story centers on horse trainer Larry Stevens (McCrea), whose last horse is in hock for a feed bill. He finds one half of a thousand dollar bill on the ground but before he can get to the other half it is picked up by Julia Wayne (Bennett), a country girl with ambition to be an actress. They unite in order to redeem the bill because they are both in need of money. Julia wants to pay off a lecherous suitor and Larry needs money to get his horse back. Complications arise when they discover that the bill is part of the proceeds from a bank robbery. They camp out in a coal yard, whose flustery old owner (Andy Clyde) harbors dreams of owning prize race horses. With his help, they manage to get Larry's horse into a race and it wins, thus solving all ther problems.

If *Two in a Crowd* is considered a 'lost' film it cannot be a matter of much concern. The reviews it received mark it as being hampered by "indifferent dialogue" and "slovenly scenario" defeating the efforts of its competent team of players. *Two in a Crowd* helps to understand why Joel McCrea started dictating the course of his career as soon as he had sufficient clout.

ADVENTURES IN MANHATTEN

Columbia, 1936;
Directed by Edward Ludwig; Written by Sydney Buchman, Harry Sauber, Jack Kirkland and Joseph Krumgold, based on the novel *Purple and Fine Linen* by May Edington; Photographed by Henry Freulich; 73 minutes.

Cast:
Claire Peyton, Jean Arthur; *George Melville*, Joel McCrea; *Blacktop Gregory*, Reginald Owen; *Phil Bane*, Thomas Mitchell; *Tim*, Herman Bing; *Mark Gibbs*, Victor Kilian; *McGuire*, John Gallaudet; *Lorimer*, Emmet Vogan; *Duncan*, George Cooper; *Philip*, Robert Warwick.

Joel McCrea's second Goldwyn loan-out was an improvement on the first and again teamed him with Jean Arthur, who now had a much more fixed image after starring with Gary Cooper in Frank Capra's *Mr. Deeds Goes to Town* (1936). With her slightly husky voice and amusingly flustered manner, she was the All-American Girl, wavering between being soft hearted and feisty. Because of her value to Columbia, to whom she was under contract, she received top billing in *Adventure in Man-*

hatten, although the role is secondary to that of McCrea, who plays a criminologist named George Melville.

Melville is hired by a newspaper to work with its editor (Thomas Mitchell) to solve a series of thefts of art treasures and famous gems. Melville is also required to write about his adventures while tracking the criminal, because he himself is an expert in art. This gives him an interesting edge in his sleuthing because he can almost predict what will be stolen next. It is this expertise that enables him to finally nab the cultivated crook, whose tastes in art are not far removed from those of Melville.

The thief, known as Blacktop Gregory (Reginald Owen), sets his sights on a robbery that requires elaborate preparation. To bring it off he becomes a theatrical producer and hires a theatre, along with actress Claire Peyton (Arthur). The theatre adjoins a bank where a celebrated diamond is kept. To get at it, Blacktop needs to blast a passage through the wall between the theatre and the bank. To cover the noise, he stages a war play, the finale of which is a battle scene. As the canons roar on stage, his men below fire their explosives. However, by this time Melville, with the help of Claire, has figured out Blacktop's scheme and foils it.

Adventures in Manhatten is an amusing minor picture, a good role for McCrea, although as scripted the role requires him to be more brilliant with his predictions that might be logical. For Jean Arthur, never a very confident actress, the choice of McCrea pleased her, and when it came time to do *The More the Merrier* that fact would come into play.

With Jean Arthur.

COME AND GET IT

United Artists, 1936;
Produced by Samuel Goldwyn; Directed by Howard
Hawks and William Wyler; Written by Jules Furthman
and Jane Murfin, based on the novel by Edna Ferber;
Photographed by Gregg Toland; Music by Alfred
Newman; 99 minutes.

Cast:
Barney Glasgow, Edward Arnold; *Richard Glasgow*, Joel
McCrea; *Lotta (mother and daughter)*, Frances Farmer;
Swan Bostrom, Walter Brennen; *Evvie Glasgow*, Andrea
Leeds; *Tony Schwerke*, Frank Shields; *Karie Linbeck*, Mady
Christians; *Emma Louise Glasgow*, Mary Nash; *Gunnar
Gallagher*, Clem Bevans; *Sid LaMaire*, Edwin Maxwell;
Josie, Cecil Cunningham; *Gubbins*, Harry Bradley;
Steward, Rollo Lloyd; *Jed Hewitt*, Charles Halton;
Goodnow, Al K. Hall.

With Frances Farmer, Walter Brennen, and Mady Christian.

Samuel Goldwyn called Joel McCrea back into the fold for his expensive filming of Edna Ferber's saga of a Wisconsin lumber dynasty, *Come and Get It*, giving him second billing in a film in which the actor does not appear until about half way through. The story spans almost fifty years in the life of an ambitious and often ruthless lumber baron named Barney Glasgow. Goldwyn wanted Spencer Tracy for this powerful role but Tracy hedged because he did not like the fact that the character dies, at least he does in the book. In the film he ends up as a bitter old man. Not about to argue the matter, Goldwyn decided to use Edward Arnold, one of the strongest and most respected character actors of Hollywood's Golden Age. Goldwyn hired Howard Hawks, the right man to direct this macho story, but interferred so much with the director that he walked off the picture before its completion. William Wyler, directing *Dodsworth* on a nearby sound stage, was brow beaten by Goldwyn into finishing *Come and Get It*, hence the highly unusual billing of co-direction by a pair of industry giants, Hawks and Wyler.

The story begins in 1884, with Glasgow a hard-driving lumber camp boss. In company with his friend and assistant Swan Bostrom (Walter Brennan), Glasgow bullies workers, brawls in saloons, charms women and generally manipulates his way to success. He falls in love with saloon singer Lotta Morgan (Frances Farmer) but dumps her in favor of a marriage that will assure him influence and power in the lumber industry. His dour wife Emma

(Mary Nash), whom he largely ignores, bears him a son, Richard (McCrea), who becomes his assistant when he reaches manhood. But Richard is an idealistic young man, with ideas more liberal than those of his brutal father.

After being cast off by Glasgow, Lotta marries Swan and they have a daughter. Some twenty years later, Glasgow, now a lumber tycoon, visits Swan and is struck by the resemblance of the daughter, also named Lotta (Also Frances Farmer), to her now deceased mother. Glasgow creates a position for Swan in his company as a way of bringing Lotta to the city. Glasgow courts the unwilling Lotta and finds an unexpected rival. Lotta and Richard fall in love, and nothing Glasgow does can break them apart. It is a fight he is bound to lose, particularly when Lotta humiliates him in front of people by calling him "an old man."

Come and Get It was a triumph for Edward Arnold. He received much critical approval but no Oscar nomination. Perhaps the Academy was confused about nominating a famous character actor in a leading role. They gave the 1936 Best Supporting Actor award to Walter Brennan for his playing of Swan Bostrum, the first of Brennan's three Oscars. The film holds up well with its solid production values, good story line and fine acting. It also affords an opportunity to study the work of the lovely but tragic Frances Farmer, as well as that of McCrea in a convincing portrayal of a sensitive yet strong young man.

BANJO ON MY KNEE

20th Century-Fox, 1936;
Produced by Darryl F. Zanuck; Directed by John
Cromwell; Written by Nunnally Johnson, based on the
novel by Harry Hamilton; Photographed by Ernest
Palmer; Music direction: Arthur Lange; Songs by Jimmy
McHugh and Harold Adamson; 95 minutes.

Cast:
Pearl Holley, Barbara Stanwyck; *Ernie Holley*, Joel
McCrea; *Grandma*, Helen Westley; *Buddy*, Buddy Ebsen;
Newt Holley, Walter Brennen; *Loota Long*, Katherine
DeMille; *Chick Bean*, Tony Martin; *Ruby*, Minna
Gombell; *Jules*, George Humbert; *Warfield Scott*, Walter
Catlett; *Judge Tope*, Spencer Charters; *Hattie*, Cecil
Weston; *Eph*, Louis Mason; *Gertha*, Hilda Vaughn; *Slade*,
Victor Kilian.

Joel McCrea was again sent to work elsewhere,
this time to 20th Century-Fox for a folksey picture
about life on the Mississippi, *Banjo on My Knee*. The
best thing about it was that it brought him together
again with Barbara Stanwyck, whose role in the
film is substantially more interesting than his. Seen
today, it provides a woefully outdated Hollywood
concept of life on the river. It protrays a small group

leading happy-go-lucky lives on "Island No. 21," a
sandbar on which they are permnanently moored,
apparently unconcerned about the rest of the
world.

The picture opens with the wedding of boat
dweller Ernie Holley (McCrea) and his girl from the
land, Pearl (Stanwyck). Presiding over the festivi-
ties is Ernie's zesty old Dad, Newt (Walter Brennan), who is anxious for the newly weds to get on
with the business of providing him with a grand-
child. When a grimey old river rat (Victor Kilian)
insists on the right to kiss the bride, Ernie wallops
him and sends him over the side of the boat. When
the man fails to surface after some minutes it is
assumed Ernie has killed him, so Ernie makes immediate plans to get away leaving his bride behind.
The man turns up a day later, but by then Ernie is
well away, and stays away for six months. When he
returns, he gets some wrong ideas about how Pearl
has been conducting herself in his absence and off
he goes again.

Pearl decides to accept the offer of a lecherous
photographer (Walter Catlett) to go to New Orleans
and become his model, although she had a change
of heart afterwards and gets a job in a restaurant

With Victor Killian and Barbara Stanwyck.

With Buddy Ebsen.

instead. She quits the restaurant to join a singer (Tony Martin) in a show. The act becomes a big success when old Newt turns up to do his One-Man-Band act. Pearl's brother Buddy (Buddy Ebsen), who amuses the crowds with his eccentric dancing, also joins the act.

When Ernie comes back to find all this, he again becomes angry, smashes up the place and gets thrown in jail. When he goes back to Island No. 21, he is persuaded by Loota Long (Katherine DeMille) that he should divorce Pearl and marry her. Newt does some fancy maneuvering to ruin that plan, resulting in the angry Loota cutting loose the Holley boat during a wild storm. The Holleys manage to save the boat from foundering by steering it onto a sandbar, after which Newt pushes Ernie and Pearl into the bedroom and nails the door shut.

Banjo on My Knee provides some light entertainment with its songs and dances and corny comedy, but it is of interst mainly for the Stanwyck performance. A former New York dancer, this was her debut in movie musical form. For McCrea it was a silly part, in which he appears somewhat ill-at-ease in his role as a riverboat hick.

INTERNS CAN'T TAKE MONEY

Paramount, 1937;
Produced by Benjamin Glazer; Directed by Alfred Santell; Written by Rian James and Theodore Reeves; Photographed by Theodore Sparkuhl; Music by Gregory Stone; 75 minutes.

Cast:
Janet Haley, Barbara Stanwyck; *Jimmie Kildare*, Joel McCrea; *Hanlon*, Lloyd Nolan; *Innes*, Stanley Ridges; *Weeks*, Lee Bowman; *Stooly Martin*, Barry Macollum; *Jeff*, Irving Bacon; *Jones*, Steve Gaylord Pendleton; *Dr. Pearson*, Pierre Watkin; *Grate*, Charles Lane; *Haines*, James Bush; *Interne*, Nick Lucats; *Eddie*, Frank Bruno; *Sister Superior*, Fay Holden.

A good Trivial Pursuit question might be: who was the first actor to play Dr. Kildare on the screen? The likely answer might be Lew Ayres, but the correct answer would be Joel McCrea. The character of the young, crusading doctor was the invention of

With Barbara Stanwyck.

novelist Max Brand, known primarily for his westerns. After making *Interns Can't Take Money*, Paramount took no further interest in the Kildare stories despite the fact that they received good reviews. MGM then bought the rights to the Kildare stories and turned them into a series of excellent B pictures starring Ayres. Although *Interns Can't Take Money* was the third pairing of McCrea with Barbara Stanwyck, it was the first time they showed how well they could act together when given the right material. Stanwyck could always rise above poor material, but McCrea could not. An excellent example of that is the comparison between this film and *Banjo on My Knee*. In *Interns Can't Take Money*, McCrea is totally credible as the no-nonsense but compassionate Kildare and Stanwyck is poignantly effective as Janet Haley, a woman going through a very difficult time in her life.

Janet emerges from jail having served a sentence for bank robbery and is brought to a clinic, having suffered an arm wound. She is examined by Kildare who immediately spots her anemic condition brought about by lack of nutrition. Later, he runs into her when he drops into a saloon for a drink where a gangster, Hanlon (Lloyd Nolan), is shot down. Realizing that only an immediate operation can save him, Kildare has Hanlon laid on a barroom table, and with Janet as an assistant, saves the man's life. When he is offered money for the operation he refuses because it is against the rules of his hospital.

Kildare begins to see more of Janet and learns that her main concern is finding her three-year-old son. All attempts end in frustration until Hanlon hears about her need, and through his connections

With Stanwyck and Lloyd Nolan.

WOMAN CHASES MAN

United Artists, 1937;
Produced by Samuel Goldwyn; Directed by John Blystone; Written by Joseph Anthony, Mannie Self and David Hertz, based on a story by Lynn Root and Frank Fenton; Photographed by Gregg Toland; Music by Alfred Newman; 71 minutes.

Cast:
Virginia Travis, Miriam Hopkins; *Kenneth Nolan*, Joel McCrea; *B. J. Nolan*, Charles Winninger; *Henri Saffron*, Erik Rhodes; *Judy Williams*, Ella Logan; *Nina Tennyson*, Leona Maricle; *Hunk Williams*, Broderick Crawford; *Mr. Judd*, Charles Halton; *Doctor*, William Jaffrey; *Taxi Driver*, George Chandler.

In the heyday of the so-called screwball comedy, Samuel Goldwyn was determined to score a success in that genre with Miriam Hopkins. He hired the top writer of the day, Ben Hecht, to write an original script. It did not meet with Goldwyn's approval, so he called in other writers until, after several treatments, he arrived at something he felt was worth shooting. Both William Wyler and Gregory LaCava refused to direct the project, and even Miriam Hopkins wanted to be assigned to something else. But Goldwyn was never a man to back down on anything he wanted to do, so he finally got John Blystone to direct and hauled in Joel McCrea to once again play opposite Hopkins - for the last time.

Woman Chases Man is about a lady architect named Virginia Travis (Hopkins) and staid young

With Miriam Hopkins.

in the underworld, locates the child, allowing Kildare and Janet find a life together.

Interns Can't Take Money is a remarkably good film of its time, due not only to the convincing work of Stanwyck and McCrea but also the frim direction of Alfred Santell, using Hans Dreier as his art director and Theodore Sparkuhl as his cameraman. The stark sets, the sharp lighting and the suspense give the film a quality beyond the norm for its modest class. It was because of the strength and the skill of her acting in this film that McCrea was moved to help Stanwyck in her desire to play *Stella Dallas*, which Samuel Goldwyn was planning to film with King Vidor as the director.

Said Stanwyck, "Joel practically clubbed Goldwyn into getting me into *Stella Dallas*." McCrea said "Vidor wanted Stanwyck from the start but Goldwyn wanted to test three or four other good actresses to be sure. Barbara didn't want to test, and I got Vidor to hold out for her if she made the test. He agreed. Then I talked her into taking it. She was far and away the best, but she shouldn't have had to test - any more than you would test Gable for a part. There is no better actress than Stanwyck if she is cast correctly. Goldwyn was a peculiar man but he made fine pictures."

millionaire, Kenneth Nolan (McCrea). Virginia, who has never let the fact that she is a woman have any bearing on her agressiveness in business, comes to the slightly daffy land developer B. J. Nolan (Charles Winninger) with a set of plans for a surburban development project, positive that it will be an enormous success. The problem is that Nolan has no money and his wealthy son, ever cautious with money, refuses to back his eccentric father. Worse than that - the old fellow is in debt and needs a large sum to hold off creditors.

In order to give the appearance of wealth and thereby raise the capitol, Virginia hires a pair of movie theatre workers (Ella Logan and Broderick Crawford) to pose as Nolan's maid and butler. Complicating the scheme is the presence of a pair of tricksters, a fortune huntress (Leona Maricle) and her fussy boyfriend (Erik Rhodes), who are trying to worm their way in with the supposedly rich old Nolan. Virginia, who needs to soften up the rigid yound Nolan in order to get him to back her project, discovers he has a weakness for champagne. She plies him with drink, but as he softens up and becomes less formal, she finds herself falling in love with him. Love eventually solves everything.

After *Woman Chases Man*, Goldwyn announced that there would be another Hopkins-McCrea vehicle, but none ever came about. Hopkins was later loaned out to RKO for *Wise Girl*, with Ray Milland, and with that she completed her Goldwyn contract. While *Woman Chases Man* was a weak ending for McCrea's teaming with Miriam Hopkins, the association was one that had done him a great deal of good. The pictures had played to big audiences and

had added to his stature and his reputation as a solidly reliable leading man. With that fact recognized by Goldwyn it was therefore recognized by all of Hollywood.

DEAD END

United Artists, 1937;
Produced by Samuel Goldwyn; Directed by William Wyler; Written by Lillian Hellman, based on the play by Sidney Kingsley; Photographed by Gregg Toland; Music by Alfred Newman; 93 minutes.

Cast:
Drina, Sylvia Sidney; *Dave Connell*, Joel McCrea; *Baby Face Martin*, Humphrey Bogart; *Kay Burton*, Wendy Barrie; *Francey*, Claire Trevor; *Hunk*, Allen Jenkins; *Mrs. Martin*, Marjorie Main; *Tommy*, Billy Halop; *Dippy*, Huntz Hall; *Angel*, Bobby Jordan; *Spit*, Leo Gorcey; *T. B.*, Gabriel Dell; *Milty*, Bernard Punsley; *Philip Griswold*, Charles Peck; *Mr. Griswold*, Minor Watson; *Officer Mulligan*, James Burke; *Doorman*, Ward Bond.

Part of Samuel Goldwyn's resolve as a film producer was to excell in every genre of film. In 1937, he decided it was time to prove his mettle in contemporary American social drama, so he purchased the rights to Sidney Kingsley's play *Dead End*. To make it as powerful as possible, he commissioned Lillian Hellman to write the screenplay and assigned it to director William Wyler. Wyler wanted to make the film even more powerful by shooting it in New York, but Goldwyn always felt that everything should be done at home base. He told his best

With Tom Tully and Humphrey Bogart.

With Sylvia Sydney.

designer, Richard Day, to fill an entire sound stage with the East Side sets called for in the story, including part of the waterfront, the back of a Sutton Place apartment building and an array of slums.

Goldwyn imported the teenage actors who played the slum kids in the Broadway production (henceworth they would become known as the Dead End Kids), along with Marjorie Main for the role of the mother of vicious gangster Baby Face Martin. To play Martin, Goldwyhn borrowed Humphrey Bogart from Warner Bros. To play the idealistic young leading man, who else on the Goldwyn lot but Joel McCrea?

The setting juxtadisposes wealth and poverty, with out-of-work, would-be architect Dave Connell (McCrea) in love with both shopgirl Drina (Silvia Sydney), striving to survive in a dingy tenement, and Kay (Wendy Barrie), the stylish Sutton Place mistress of a racketeer. Dave dreams of designing buildings to replace the slums where he grew up. Back to this drab locale comes Baby Face Martin, mostly to see his impoverished mother and his former girlfriend Francey (Claire Trevor). He finds Francey making a living as a prostitute and a mother who wants nothing to do with him. She turns down his money, slaps his face and tells him he is an animal.

Dave warns Martin to get out and leave alone the street kids who idolize him because of his success as a criminal. When Martin kidnaps a rich boy,

Philip Griswold (Charles Peck), Dave tries to intercede but is knifed and pushed into the river. He survives, and after taking a gun from Martin's henchman Hunk (Allen Jenkins), pursues Martin and kills him. The shabby, cowardly ending of Martin disillusions the street kids; Kay decides her best choice is to leave town with the man who keeps her; and Dave decides Drina is the girl for him. Together they will do what they can to make a good life and help the community.

Dead End was well received by the critics who felt Goldwyn had made all the right points dramatically and socially. Wyler maintained that he could have made it even stronger had he used genuine New York locations instead of a somewhat sanitized set. However, that set is a marvel of design and brought Richard Day an Oscar nomination. The film was nominated as one of the best of 1937, but lost to *The Life of Emile Zola*. Claire Trevor was nominated as Best Supporting Actress. In retrospect, it is difficult to understand how the superb performance of Marjorie Main was overlooked in that same category. Gregg Toland, who photographed most of Goldwyn's best films, was nominated for his splendidly probing, subtly shadowed lensing of *Dead End* but the Academy members that year voted in favor of Karl Freund's work on *The Good Earth*. However, the much nominated Toland did receive an Oscar in 1939, for Goldwyn's *Wuthering Heights*.

For McCrea, *Dead End* was yet one more instance of "good old, reliable Joel," the unflappable, rock solid leading man.

WELLS FARGO

Paramount, 1937;
Produced and directed by Frank Llyoyd; Written by Paul Schofield, Gerald Geraghty and Frederick Jackson, based on a story by Stuart Lake; Photographed by Theodore Sparkuhl; Music by Victor Young; 115 minutes.

Cast:
Ramsay McKay, Joel McCrea; *Justine Pryor*, Frances Dee; *Hank York*, Bob Burns; *Dal Slade*, Lloyd Nolan; *Henry Wells*, Henry O'Neill; *Mrs. Pryor*, Mary Nash; *Nicholas Pryor*, Ralph Morgan; *Talbot Carter*, Johnny Mack Brown; *James Oliver*, Porter Hall; *William Fargo*, Jack Clark; *John Butterfield*, Clarence Kolb; *Dan Trimball*, Robert Cummings; *Alice McKay*, Peggy Stewart; *Pawnee*, Bernard Siegel; *Abe*, Stanley Fields; *Lucy Dorset*, Jane Dewey; *Abraham Lincoln*, Frank McGlynn.

With Frances Dee and Mary Nash.

Despite his later image as a movie westerner - and the one by which he is best remembered - Joel McCrea did not appear in a western film until eight years after becoming a Hollywood leading man. Producer-director Frank Lloyd (1888-1960), long known for his historical epics, asked Paramount to sign McCrea for the film he wanted to make about the express and transportation company set up by Henry Wells and William Fargo in 1852. The end result, *Wells Fargo*, was a handsome, broad treatment somewhat hampered by being overly respectful and a little ponderous. It is the kind of Americana epic film long out of favor. Originally released at almost two-hours, subsequent reissues cut it by as much as half an hour in order to make it seem more exciting.

The sprawling story starts in 1843, in Batavia, New York, then the most westwardly point on the railroad. Energetic and enterprising young Ramsay McKay (McCrea) throws himself wholeheartedly behind the ambitions of his employers, Henry Wells (Henry O'Neill) and William Fargo (Jack Clark). He is entrusted with their most important missions and while on one of them he comes to the aid of Justine Pryor (Frances Dee) and her mother (Mary Nash) when their buggy breaks down. The Pryors are southern aristocrats. On a trip to St. Louis, McKay again meets Justine and they fall in love, despite the objections of her haughty mother. When McKay is

68

With Stanley Fields.

With Lloyd Nolan and Porter Hall.

transferred to California to supervise business in the newly found gold fields, Justine decides to follow him.

McKay and Justine marry and live happily despite the rough environment and the opposition of her parents. Congress grants Wells Fargo a contract for overland mail and the Pony Express is established. Lincoln is elected President and the Civil War errupts.

After Confederate soldiers rob several Federal gold shipments, McKay is put in charge of a huge consignment. Mrs. Pryor, who had come to stay with Justine to help with the birth of a child, goads Justine into protesting against her husband's support for the Union cause. Justine, whose brother has been killed fighting for the Confederacy, overhears McKay making his plans and writes down the route he will take. She tells him that if he undertakes the assignment it will mean the end of their marriage. He tells her he has no choice. She, however, cannot conspire against him and throws away the paper on which she had noted his route.

McKay's gold train is attacked by a Confederate calvary force under the command of Talbot Carter (Johnny Mack Brown), a friend of Justine's. The attack is routed and Carter is killed. In his wallet McKay finds Justine's note, which her mother had picked up and sent to Carter. After the war the embittered McKay devotes all his time to business.

After many years of service, Wells Fargo gives a banquet of appreciation in honor of McKay. Afterwards he returns to his hotel fo find his daughter

Alice (Peggy Stewart) waiting for him. She asks him to attend her seventeenth birthday party the next day. He at first refuses, knowing Justine will be there, but later changes his mind. Brought together by Alice, McKay and Justine agree that they should put their troubles behind them. As a token of that McKay hands Justine the note he found on Carter's body. Surprised, she explains that she threw it away and that the only way it could have reached Carter was by her embittered mother. The two now realize the cause of their estrangement and agree to spend the rest of their lives together.

Joel McCrea looks back on *Wells Fargo* with particular affection. Not only was it his first movie epic, it also co-starred him with wife Frances Dee in a story of romance and spectacle. He also regards it fondly because of the Scots-born Frank Lloyd. In Hollywood since 1913, Lloyd won the first of his two Oscars for direction for *Divine Lady* (1929), a story about Admiral Lord Nelson and his love for Emma Hamilton. In 1933 he won another for *Cavalcade*, and two years later received a nomination for *Mutiny on the Bounty*. Says McCrea, "I learned more about integrity and sincerity from Frank Lloyd than from anybody else. When he was working he was just like a general, he was meticulous, he took full responsibility for planning and he was always on time. At the start of each day he would explain to the whole cast and crew just what it was he was hoping to achieve that day. I had lunch with him one day and was a little late. He said, 'Laddie, when you tell a person you're going to meet them somewhere, do your utmost to be on time. Be able to be counted upon.'"

McCrea was a pallbearer at Lloyd's funeral. "He was a great friend and everyone was important to him. I remember Gable telling me, 'When I was doing *Mutiny on the Bounty*, he was my saving grace.' Everybody felt that way about him. He's not as well remembered as some of the other directors, maybe because he wasn't so colorful but he was a fine, dignified man."

THREE BLIND MICE

20th Century-Fox, 1938;
Produced by Darryl F. Zanuck; Directed by William A. Seiter; Written by Brown Holmes and Lynn Starling, based on a play by Stephen Powys; Photographed by Ernest Palmer; Music direction: Arthur Lange; 75 minutes.

Cast:
Pamela Charters, Loretta Young; *Van Smith*, Joel McCrea; *Steve Harrington*, David Niven; *Mike Brophy*, Stuart

With David Niven and Loretta Young.

Erwin; *Moira Charters*, Marjorie Weaver; *Elizabeth Charters*, Pauline Moore; *Miriam*, Binnie Barnes; *Mrs. Kilian*, Jane Darwell; *Young Man*, Leonid Kinskey; *Hendricks*, Spencer Charters; *Clerk*, Franklin Pangborn.

One of the basic plots in the heyday of the Hollywood screwball comedy was the one about the poor girl in search of a rich husband. *Three Blind Mice* is the example par excellence, so much so that after gaining the rights to the Stephen Powys play, 20th Century Fox used the plot in several other films. In 1941 it became the Betty Grable musical *Moon Over Miami*; in 1946 it evolved into the June Haver musical *Three Little Girls in Blue*; and in 1953 it was reworked for *How to Marry a Millionaire*, not to mention other scenarios which would appear to have their roots in the Powys play. In 1938, it provided Joel McCrea with his only chance to play leading man to the delightful Loretta Young.

The setting is Santa Barbara, California, and the film gives an interesting backward glance at that fashionable and affluent town with its resort hotels, beaches and playgrounds. Into this pleasant environment come three sisters from Kansas, Pamela Charters (Young), Moira (Marjorie Weaver) and Elizabeth (Pauline Moore). Having come into a small family legacy, they use the money to finance a trip with the specific purpose of locating potential wealthy husbands. To do this Pamela poses as a rich socialite, with the sisters pretending to be her secretary and maid. Pamela is soon pursued by two handsome prospects. One is Van Smith (McCrea), the scion of a blue book family but at the moment, a man with more genealogy than cash. After a lot of enjoyable flirtation, the truth comes out, and Pamela admits that she, too, has limited funds. They part company, thinking it better to go their own ways.

Pamela next turns to the suitor with the money, Steve Harrington (David Niven), a rancher with mountain estates and a willingness to wed. But Pamela knows the marriage will be a mistake because her heart is not in it; her heart is yearning for Van. The solution for Steve is easily arrived at when he finds Elizabeth is not Pamela's secretary but her sister. Meanwhile, sister Moira makes a nice discovery when it turns out that the bartender (Stuart Erwin) who has been paying her attention is actually a millionaire. This leaves Pamela and Van to come to their senses and realize that their feelings for each other are more important than money.

Three Blind Mice is slick Hollywood entertainment at its 1938 best, with good production values, snappy dialogue, glib humor and pleasing sets and costumes, all of which gives the impression that California is a land of romance, soft music, moonlight and abundance. The cast is excellent, with Loretta Young at the peak of her young and stylish beauty, David Niven gradually emerging as an appealing, amusing leading man, and Joel McCrea revealing a talent for light comedy. One of the people who spotted that talent and would soon enlarge it was Preston Sturges.

YOUTH TAKES A FLING

Universal, 1938;
Produced by Joe Pasternak; Directed by Archie Mayo; Written by Myles Connolly, based on a story by Elliott Gibbons; Photographed by Rudolph Mate; 77 minutes.

Cast:
Joe Meadows, Joel McCrea; *Helen Brown,* Andrea Leeds; *Frank,* Frank Jenks; *Jean,* Dorothea Kent; *Mrs. Merrivale,* Isabel Jeans; *Madge,* Virginia Grey; *Mrs. Duke,* Grant Mitchell; *Dunham,* Henry Mollison; *Tad,* Brandon Tynan; *Captain Walters,* Oscar O'Shea; *Mr. Judd,* Granville Bates; *Floorwalker,* Roger Davis; *George,* Willie Best.

The least impressive of Joel McCrea's films of the Thirties are those he made at Universal, mostly on loan-out from either RKO or Samuel Goldwyn. *Youth Takes a Fling,* for which Goldwyn not only loaned McCrea but his starlet Andrea Leeds, is only a little above McCrea's Universal average. It has McCrea as a young man - now at thirty-three, he

With Andrea Leeds.

was already getting a little too old for this fluff - from Kansas who has a hankering to go to sea and be a sailor. In New York he finds no shipping company willing to offer him a berth, so he takes a job as a truck driver with a large department store.

Friendly, innocent Joe Meadows (McCrea) is soon spotted by one of the store's prettiest clerks, Helen Brown (Leeds), who decides Joe is the man for her. To this end she enlists the help of her fellow employees, friends Frank (Frank Jenks) and Jean (Dorothea Kent), to help her snare the unwilling Joe. He brushes her off at every turn, until her romantic overtures finally cause him to give in.

In his book *The Universal Story* (Crown, 1983), Clive Hirschorn makes a good point about this minor entry in the history of screen romances, describing it as "A comedy clearly designed to confirm a misogynist's most fearful prejudices." Fortunately for McCrea, a really good movie was about to elevate his standing at the box office.

UNION PACIFIC

Paramount, 1939;
Produced and directed by Cecil B. DeMille; Written by Walter DeLeon, C. Gardner Sullivan and Jesse Lasky, Jr., based on the novel *Trouble Shooter* by Ernest Haycox; Photographed by Victor Milner and Dewey Wrigley; Music by Sigmund Krumgold; 135 minutes.

Cast:
Mollie Monahan, Barbara Stanwyck; *Jeff Butler,* Joel McCrea; *Fiesta,* Akim Tamiroff; *Dick Allen,* Robert Preston; *Leach Overmile,* Lynne Overman; *Sid Campeau,* Brian Donlevy; *Duke Ring,* Robert Barrat; *Cordray,* Anthony Quinn; *Casement,* Stanley Ridges; *Asa M. Barrows,* Henry Kolker; *Grenville N. Dodge,* Francis McDonald; *Oakes Ames,* Willard Robertson; *Calvin,* Harold Goodwin; *Mrs. Calvin,* Evelyn Keyes; *Sam Reed,* Richard Lane; *Dusky Clayton,* William Haade; *Paddy O'Rourke,* Regis Toomey; *Monahan,* J. M. Kerrigan; *Cookie,* Fuzzy Knight; *Al Brett,* Harry Woods; *Dollarhide,* Lon Chaney, Jr.; *General U. S. Grant,* Joseph Crehan.

When Cecil B. DeMille asked Joel McCrea if he would like to play the lead in *Union Pacific,* McCrea replied, "You'd be better off with Cooper." DeMille explained that Cooper was tied up with other commitments for quite some while, and repeated his question. McCrea said he would gladly do it. "He sent me the script, I read it and that's how I got *Union Pacific.*"

DeMille had announced his intentions to make

the film while directing Gary Cooper in *The Plainsman* (1937). First he had to finish his production of another episode of American history, *The Buccaneer*, with Fredric March as the French pirate Jean Lafitte, who helped the American beat the British at the Battle of New Orleans in 1815. With that epic under his belt, he then enlisted the cooperation of the Union Pacific Railroad in telling the story of the first transcontinental train service in America. It would be by a love story, plus scenes of gun fights, saloon brawls, Indian raids, cavalry rescue, the demolition of a gambling pest hole by vigilantes and a train wreck. With the kind of preparation that was his hallmark, DeMille asked the Union Pacific to provide all the historical research they could muster, as well as the use of old trains and the crews to work them.

The film opens with a conference in Washington, D.C., where politicians and railroad executives agree that a coast-to-coast railroad is now essential. Later, one of the sponsors of the project agrees to be part of the sabotaging of the Union Pacific's interest in favor of a rival company. This opposition is soon apparent in the labor camps with fights and unrest.

Sent by the government to obviate such movements is Jeff Butler (McCrea), well known as a railroad "trouble shooter." He quickly sizes up Sid Campeau (Brian Donlevy), who operates the gambling saloon, as the primary source of conflict. Butler also meets Mollie Monahan (Barbara Stanwyck), the post mistress who dispatches mail from the end of the line, wherever that may be. Mollie is being courted by charming young scalawag Dick Allen (Robert Preston), an old friend of Butler's from army days. Butler soon learns Allen is in cahoots with Campeau to stir up trouble with the men by providing such distractions as gambling, liquor and dance hall girls.

The company pay train is robbed by Allen and a gang, and he takes the money bags to Mollie's accomodation. Butler soon arrives, having trailed Allen, but Mollie covers for Allen, claiming that he had been with her and that they are planning to marry. Later she persuades Allen to return the money, which leads to her dismissal from the Postal Service. She and Allen leave on a train but it is attacked by Indians who wreck it and kill the crew and passengers. Butler is also on the train and he joins Allen and Mollie in a section of the wreck, hoping the Indians will overlook them. But the Indians find them, and just as Butler prepares to use his last bullet to kill Mollie, a cavalry unit arrives to save them.

With Robert Preston and Brian Donlevy.

With Barbara Stanwyck and Preston.

With Stanwyck.

Allen, no longer wishing to be a part of the sabotage, faces Campeau and is killed. Butler soon arrives on the scene and kills Campeau. In the finale the golden spike is driven at Promontory Point with President U.S. Grant in attendance. As the Union Pacific is linked with the Central Pacific, Butler and Mollie make plans for the future.

Union Pacific is historically accurate in the main but, as with all DeMille accounts of history, it is elaborately dressed up with fictional decorations. The object was to entertain and in that regard it was a smash hit for Paramount - a lavish slice of romantic, dramatic Americana done with DeMillian style. Also it was a big hit for Joel McCrea whose career at this point needed a lift. Playing leading man to even the best of Hollywood's glamorous ladies was starting to wear a bit thin for both the actor and the public.

In order to get McCrea from Goldwyn, Paramount had to loan Dorothy Lamour for Goldwyn's *The Hurricane*, a film that McCrea avoided doing by convincing director John Ford that he was completely wrong for it. McCrea was now about to surprise even Cecil B. DeMille, whose next project was *Northwest Mounted Police*. DeMille asked McCrea if he would be interested in playing the leading role of the Texas Ranger who goes to Canada and cooperates with the Mounties. McCrea said he did not think he was right for the part and suggested it was perfect for Gary Cooper. DeMille

found that he could get Cooper, thereby for once reversing the usual business of, "If you can't get Cooper, get McCrea."

The first day on the set of *Union Pacific*, DeMille introduced McCrea to the cast and crew as "my former newsboy." Despite the fashinable tendency to downplay DeMille as a director-producer, McCrea spoke highly of him. "He was a very interesting man. Most people thought he was kind of cold and only did bathtub scenes but he had sensitivity and he was good with a lot of people, he knew how to handle people. He was a showman, like P. T. Barnum, and I enjoyed working with him. He did some good pictures, he couldn't have lasted if he hadn't. He once told me, 'The critics don't like my pictures but the public do.' He was right."

THEY SHALL HAVE MUSIC

United Artists, 1939;
Produced by Samuel Goldwyn; Directed by Archie Mayo; Written by Irmgard von Cube and John Howard Larson, based on the adaptation by Robert Presnell and Anthony Veiller of the novel by Charles L. Clifford; Photographed by Gregg Toland; Music director: Alfred Newman; 101 minutes.

Cast:
Jascha Heifetz, Himself; *Peter McCarthy,* Joel McCrea; *Ann Lawson,* Andrea Leeds; *Professor Lawson,* Walter Brennen; *Frankie,*Gene Reynolds; *Dominick,* Terry Kilburn; *Mr. Flower,* Porter Hall; *Willie,* Tommy Kelly; *Fever Jones,* Chuck Stubbs; *Rocks Mulligan,* Walter Tetley; *Betty,*Jacqueline Nash; *(later Gale Sherwood) Susie,* Mary Ruth; *Ed Miller,* Arthur Hohl; *Jane Miller,* Marjorie Main.

Joel McCrea's final film for Samuel Goldwyn was one in which he was used only for his name value and because he was under contract. Goldwyn, who always had a feeling for culture and quality, wanted to do a film about serious music and persuaded the great violinist Jascha Heifetz to make his film debut in this movie. Heifetz was a difficult man to get to do things in which he had less than a total commitment but he found, as did many others, that Samuel Goldwyn was not a man who took "no" for an answer. What finally emerged as *They Shall Have Music* took a year of changing script concepts before its release in July of 1939. During this time Heifetz became impatient with the varying starting dates given him. He agreed to a month's work at the studio, including the performance of a half-dozen pieces of music for a fee of $70,000, but he was paid another $50,000 when Goldwyn brought him back to the studio for pick-up sequences. In the film Heifetz appears as himself and is convinced to help the poor musician children in an almost destitute music school.

At the core of the story is the school run by the kindly, dedicated but impecunious Professer Lawson (Walter Brennan). His daughter Ann (Andrea Leeds) is engaged to a musically sympathetic business man, Peter McCarthy (McCrea). All of the children come from impoverished families. One of them, a tough, near-delinguent named Frankie (Gene Reynolds) discovers the beauty of music when he sneaks into Carnegie Hall and hears Jascha Heifetz. Now he wants to be a violinist, and finds a spiritual home in the orchestra of Professor Lawson. Later, when Frankie understands that the school is about to fold for lack of funds, he and some of his roughneck chums come up with the idea of persuading Heifetz to come to the school and perform with the orchestra. The great man agrees but then finds that his priceless Stradivarius has been stolen. Frankie and the kids track the culprit and get it back, and Heifetz performs the concert that saves the school.

The critics liked *They Shall Have Music* more than did the public, who had to be bamboozled with advertising playing up the adventures of the roughneck kids rather than Heifetz. Aside from concert performances in two other films (*Carnegie Hall* and *Of Men and Music*) this was his only acting performance and is therefore of interest historically. Apart

With Walter Brennen, Jacqueline Nash, and Andrea Leeds.

from that it is a musically pleasing film, with a range of good performances for which music director Alfred Newman won an Oscar nomination.

For Joel McCrea it was simply a walk-through, and one that concluded his contract with Goldwyn. The association had been a good one for him but he felt it had limitations, especially now that he had scored with his work in *Union Pacific*. By this time in his career McCrea was bolder about deciding what he wanted to do and what he did not. He had offended Goldwyn by not playing the lead in *The Hurricane*, and there would doubtlessly be more altercations like that. It was time to move on.

ESPIONAGE AGENT

Warner Bros, 1939;
Produced by Louis F. Edelman; Directed by Lloyd Bacon; Written by Warren Duff, Michael Fessler and Frank Donaghue, based on the story *Career Man* by Robert Buckner; Photographed by Charles Rosher; Music by Adolph Deutsch; 83 minutes.

Cast:
Barry Corvall, Joel McCrea; *Brenda Ballard*, Brenda Marshall; *Lowell Warington*, Jeffrey Lynn; *Dudley Garrett*, George Bancroft; *Hamilton Peyton*, Stanley Ridges; *Dr. Rader*, James Stephenson; *Walter Forbes*, Howard Hickman; *Mrs. Corvall*, Nana Bryant; *Paul Strawn*, Robert O. Davis; *Dr. Helm*, Hans von Twardowsky; *Decker*, Lucien Prival; *Bruce Corvall*, Addison Richards; *Secretary of State*, Edwin Stanley.

Warner Bros., the most obvious of the studios in its warning about the Nazi menace, had cogently sounded that alarm with *The Confessions of a Nazi Spy*, released in May of 1939, *Espionage Agent* released in late September of 1939, appeared like a spin-off, but the thesis was narrower and the material less controversial. 1939 viewers probably found the information given about the State Department interesting, albeit somewhat confusing due to the necessary secrecy shrouding most of its operations regarding espionage, sabotage and international spying. For Joel McCrea it was a good fling at playing a State Department hero.

Barry Corvall (McCrea), a career diplomat, finds that his lovely bride Brenda (Brenda Marshall) is, or had been, a German-employed spy. This is additionally irksome because his widowed mother (Nana Bryant) reveres the memory of her dedicated

With Brenda Marshall and Jeffrey Lynn.

Crea, because it was his work in this movie that convinced Alfred Hitchcock that he was the right actor to play the lead in *Foreign Correspondent*.

HE MARRIED HIS WIFE

20th Century-Fox, 1940;
Produced by Darryl F. Zanuck; Directed by Roy Del Ruth; Written by Sam Hellman, Darrell Ware, Lynn Starling and John O'Hara, based on a story by Erna Lazarus and Scott Darling; Photographed by Ernest Palmer; Music by David Buttolph; 83 minutes.

Cast:
T. H. Randall, Joel McCrea; *Valerie,* Nancy Kelly; *Bill Carter,* Roland Young; *Ethel,* Mary Boland; *Freddie,* Cesar Romero; *Doris,* Mary Healy; *Paul Hunter,* Lyle Talbot; *Dicky Brown,* Elisha Cook, Jr.; *Huggins,* Barnet Parker; *Prisoner,* Harry Hayden; *Warden,* Charles Wilson; *Detective,* Charles D. Brown; *Mayor,* Spencer Charters.

Hoping to repeat the success they had had with *Three Blind Mice,* 20th Century Fox brought Joel McCrea back to do another comedy romance, *He Married His Wife,* but sadly without the same results. Had he been given Loretta Young as a co-star it might have worked better but with Nancy Kelly, an admirable but far less charismatice actress, the picture lacked the necessary sparkle. It also lacked a script as good as that of *Three Blind Mice.*

In this mildly amusing marital farce, McCrea is T.H. Randall, a well-heeled businessman, whose

diplomat husband. Brenda, as it turns out, is wholeheartedly American in her ideals and helps her husband obtain files of Nazi-incriminating evidence. The plot rotates around Nazi efforts to gain possession of the American industrial mobilization plans, with the goal of dynamiting the key centers of American mechanization, when and if signalled from Berlin.

Following a film technique for which Warners was well known by 1939, *Espionage Agent* mixes footage of newsreel and educational material with its fictional passages. Much of the action takes place in the halls and chambers of the State Department and one of the actors even plays the Secretary of State. The film understandably bangs the drum for what was then American foreign policy, with much lauding of the consular service. As much, it is an interesting item for study about America's, or more particularly, Hollywood's attitude toward the world of 1939.

Although he had no way of knowing at the time, *Espionage Agent* was an important film for Joel Mc-

With Charles D. Brown and Nancy Kelly.

passion for horse racing causes his wife Valerie (Kelly) to sue for divorce, despite the fact that she still loves him. After the divorce Randall is shocked by the amount of the alimony and goes to jail rather than pay it. Once out, he instructs his wily lawyer, Bill Carter (Roland Young) to maneuver Valerie into another marriage. They decide that Randall's old playboy friend Paul Hunter (Lyle Talbot) is the best candidate. When Valerie discovers the plan she makes a few maneuvers of her own.

During a weekend at the posh country estate of Carter's friend Ethel (Mary Boland), Randall does his best to push Hunter into the arms of his ex-wife. When a slick, money-hungry Lothario (Cesar Romero) makes an obvious play for Valerie, Randall finally realizes his best plan is to re-marry his ex. He also realizes that he loves her and needs to pay her at least as much attention as he does his horses. Randall also discovers that his droll attorney has been in league with Valerie to get them back together. With that, *He Married His Wife* comes to its limp but cheerful ending.

PRIMROSE PATH

RKO, 1940;
Produced and directed by Gregory La Cava; Written by Allen Scott and Gregory La Cava, based on the play by Robert L. Buckner and Wallace Hart, and the novel *February Hill* by Victoria Lincoln; Photographed by Joseph H. August; Music by Werner R. Heymann; 92 minutes.

Cast:
Ellie May Adams, Ginger Rogers; *Ed Wallace*, Joel McCrea; *Mamie Adams*, Majorie Rambeau; *Gramp*, Henry Travers; *Homer*, Miles Mander; *Grandma*, Queenie Vassar; *Honeybell*, Joan Carroll; *Thelma*, Vivienne Osborne; *Carmelita*, Carmen Morales.

Ginger Rogers' career had advanced by leaps and bounds since making *Chance in Heaven* with Joel McCrea in 1933. Not only had she made the enchanting musicals with Fred Astaire but she had also starred in comedic and dramatic material like *Stage Door* (1937), *Vivacious Lady* (1938), and *Bachelor Mother* (1939), all for RKO. The studio now gave her her best opportunity as an actress, in the film version of what had been a controversial novel and play, *February Hill*, retitled *Primrose Path* for the screen. In order to transfer it to the screen, consider-

With Ginger Rogers.

able changes were made to meet the censorial dictates of 1940. The original story dealt with a family in which prostitution has been a trade for several generations. In the film the Adams are shantytown dwellers whose sparse income is unspecified.

Ginger Rogers was the obvious choice for *Primrose Path*, but according to Joel McCrea, he was not RKO's first choice as leading man. He claimed that a famous actor, whose name he would not divulge, was signed by the studio but dismissed by director Gregory La Cava, who wanted McCrea. The other actor apparently sensed that the film was a vehicle for Rogers and wanted his part built up. La Cava, who was the producer as well as the director, asked RKO to pay the actor his full salary and then proceeded with McCrea.

McCrea's role is that of Ed Wallace, the happy-go-lucky operator of a combined gas station and cafe in a seaside California town. One day while riding his motor bike he picks up Ellie May Adams (Rogers), who is on her way to the beach to dig clams. His cheerful, confident manner wins over this rather dour girl in her late teens, and Ed gradually comes to love her without knowing much about her shabby home life. Her mother (Marjorie Rambeau) is a woman of easy virtue, her father (Miles Mander) is an alcoholic, and her grandmother (Queenie Vassar) is a crude old harridan with nothing good to say about anything.

To get away from her environment, Ellie May leads Ed toward marriage. She genuinely loves him and together they enjoy a good life, with Ellie May

With Joan Carroll, Queenie Vasar, Marjorie Rambeau, and Miles Mander.

becoming an excellent waitress and co-worker with her husband. When Ed finally meets his in-laws he is far from impressed but it has no bearing upon his regard for Ellie May. Rumors about how her mother earns her money, which is how her grandmother used to do it, gradually eat away at the marriage and lead to a separation. The death of her father and the need to support her family then lead Ellie May to the "escort" business. One evening she turns up with a "date" at a dance at which Ed is also in attendance. A fight almost ensues, but ironically it is the man who is with Ellie May who spots the bond between she and Ed and brings about a reconciliation.

Despite the strictures of production codes of 1940, *Primrose Path* is an effective and touching drama, thanks to the skill of director La Cava, along with the moody photography of Joseph H. August. All of the exteriors were shot on location around Monterey. But the film belongs to Ginger Rogers. Twenty-nine at the time, she appears in the early sequences as a tomboyish teenager, her face scrubbed clean and her eyes suggesting both defiance and vulnerability. Late in 1940, Rogers starred as *Kitty Foyle*, which brought her an Oscar as the Best Actress of that year. According to Joel McCrea, "I think they really gave it to her for *Primrose Path* but they were afraid of the subject matter in those days. Even Frank Capra said it was a better film than *Kitty Foyle*."

FOREIGN CORRESPONDENT

United Artists, 1940;
Produced by Walter Wanger; Directed by Alfred
Hitchcock; Written by Charles Bennett and Joan
Harrison, based on the book *Personal History* by Vincent
Sheean; Photographed by Rudy Mate; Music by Alfred
Newman; 119 minutes.

Cast:
Johnny Jones, Joel McCrea; *Carol Fisher,* Laraine Day;
Stephen Fisher, Herbert Marshall; *Scott ffolliott,* George
Sanders; *Van Meer,* Albert Bassermann; *Stebbins,* Robert
Benchley; *Rowley,* Edmund Gwenn; *Krug,* Edwardo
Ciannelli; *Tramp,* Martin Kosleck; *Mr. Powers,* Harry
Davenport; *Doreen,* Barbara Pepper.

In discussing *Foreign Correspondent* with fellow
director Francis Truffaut, Alfred Hitchcock pointed
out that Joel McCrea was not his choice for the lead.
He wanted Gary Cooper, who said the part did not
interest him, but later admitted the decision was a
mistake. Cooper thought it would be a routine spy
thriller, not the stylish suspense film it turned out to
be. Apparently Cooper was unfamiliar with the stylish suspense films Hitchcock had been making in
England throughout the Thirties. Hitchcock's associate producer Joan Harrison, who was also a co-
writer on this project, suggested McCrea, following
what had become almost a Hollywood law by this
time, "When you can't get Cooper, get McCrea."
She had seen him in *Espionage Agent* and felt he
would be good as the American reporter who gets

With Laraine Day.

mixed up in European political intrigue. Hitchcock's reason for wanting Cooper was that he felt
the role should be played by a bedrock American
type, not a sophisticated or subtly humorous actor
of the Cary Grant school. There was an underlying
reason for this; *Foreign Correspondent* was part of
Hollywood's none-too-subtle pre-Pearl Harbor
campaign to make the American public aware of
the Nazi menace, and pitting a solid Cooper-
McCrea type against the devious, malevolent
Hitlerian forces was clearly felt to be a point maker.

Pitting innocence against malevolence had long
been a Hitchcock device and would become more
so in later films. Here, the reporter, Johnny Jones, is
not exactly an innocent man. Indeed, he has had a
lot of experience as a hard-headed crime journalist.
He also knows what is going on in Europe in the
summer of 1939, between pro- and anti-Nazi fac-
tions. He accepts his editor's offer to go to Europe
and adopts the name of Huntley Haverstock, thinking it more elegant for a foreign correspondent. In
London, he joins Stebbins (Robert Benchley, who
was encouraged to write his own acerbic dialogue),
the paper's resident editor, who assigns him to Amsterdam - right after Jones has survived an attempt
on his life. It is, he realizes, no mere assignment.

In Amsterdam, Jones meets veteran Dutch diplomat Van Meer (Albert Bassermann), who has mem-
orized the contents of a secret treaty between
Holland and the British-French allies. Traveling
with Van Meer is an elegant Englishman, Stephen
Fisher (Herbert Marshall), the leader of a group of
pacifists, and his daughter Carol (Laraine Day). Van
Meer proceeds to where he is to make a speech
about the Nazi war plans and how war can be
averted. On the steps of the building, before a large
crowd of spectators, he is assassinated. Jones spots
the assassin and follows him to a windmill in the
country. There Jones discovers that Van Meer is
alive, a captive of the Nazis, and that it was a
double who was murdered. Jones tells this to an
English reporter friend, Scott ffollott (George Sanders) and to Carol, with whom he is now becoming
romantically involved.

The scene shifts back to London, where the Nazis
have taken Van Meer and where the two reporters
trace him and rescue him. It now becomes apparent
that Carol's father is not a pacifist but a Nazi involved in the Van Meer plot. Fisher escapes with his
daughter, who is both confused by the situation and
disillusioned by Jones.

With the outbreak of the war the Fishers board
an air liner for America. Jones and ffolliott manage

With Albert Basselman.

to get passage. The reporters confront Fisher with his duplicity but the discussions are interupted by the sound of gunfire. The plane is being fired upon by a German ship below. Direct hits cause the plane to crash into the ocean and those who survive cling to wreckage. Fisher, knowing his career is over and not wanting to embarrass the daughter he loves, slips away to his death before an American ship picks up the survivors. When Jones asks for permission to report his story the request is denied. Instead ffolliott takes a personal call, actually to the editor, and Jones, standing near the phone, loudly relates to the ship's captain what has happened. The story goes through.

Foreign Correspondent was Hitchcock's second American film, following *Rebecca*, which won the Oscar for Best Film of 1940. *Foreign Correspondent* was also nominated in the same category at the same time but there was never any doubt about which Hitchcock entry would win. It won no Oscars but garnered several nominations, including one for Albert Bassermann as Best Supporting Actor. Rudolph Mate was nominated for his photography but lost to George Barnes for *Rebecca*; Alexander Golitzen was nominated for Art Direction but lost to Cedric Gibbons and Paul Groesse for *Pride and Prejudice*; and Paul Eagler and Thomas T. Moulton were nominated for Special Effects but lost to Lawrence Butler and Jack Whitney for *Thief of Badgad*. That the film won in none of its nominated categories for technical achievements is regretable because each was a master touch in what was Hitchcock's finest constructed film to that point.

Hitchcock had been given a budget of a million and a half dollars, the biggest he had ever worked

with and the largest ever spent in Hollywood on a film of this kind. Huge sets were built to represent portions of London and Amsterdam. The assassination of Van Meer on the steps of a public building was one the of the most memorable sequences in any Hitchcock film. Filmed in pouring rain in a nightime setting and with everyone carrying an umbrella, Hitchcock cleverly shoots the escape of the assassin from a high camera angle, with the umbrellas bobbing like wet, black mushrooms marking his path. Also impressive is the set containing the windmill, with McCrea creeping around it trying to find Van Meer and elude capture. However, the scenic tour de force is the crash of the air liner into the ocean, with the descent seen from the cockpit of the plane.

For Joel McCrea the film proved that he was more than a pleasing leading man and it led to several more films of equal importance. In discussing the film years later with Truffaut, Hitchcock said that he considered McCrea too "easy going" for the role, touching upon the very image that had kept McCrea a popular film figure all through the Thirties. Despite that reservation, it did not stop *Foreign Correspondent* from becoming a great success at the box office and from being a fondly remembered Hitchcock film.

McCrea, who in private could do a fair impression of Hitchcock's speech and posture, recalls that the sometimes petulant director treated him well. "He was good to me and he surrounded me with good actors. We got along well. He had a habit of drinking champagne for lunch and I remember one day after lunch we shot a boring scene with me just standing there talking. After it was over I expected

With Laraine Day and player.

80

With George Sanders.

to hear him call 'cut,' but I looked over and he was sleeping, snoring with his lips sticking out. I called for the cut, he woke up and asked if the scene was good. I said, 'The best in the picture,' and he said, 'Print it.'"

REACHING FOR THE SUN

Paramount, 1941;
Produced and directed by William Wellman; Written by W. L. River, based on the novel *F. O. B. Detroit* by Wessel Smitter; Photographed by William C. Mellor; Music by Victor Young; 90 minutes.

Cast:
Russ Elliot, Joel McCrea; *Rita*, Ellen Drew; *Benny Morgan*, Eddie Bracken; *Herman*, Albert Dekker; *Amos*, Billy Gilbert; *Jerry*, George Chandler; *Rita's mother*, Bodil Ann Rosing; *Norm*, James Burke; *Johnson*, Charles D. Brown; *Landlady*, Elly Malyon.

Dealing as it does with the contrast between country life and life in the car factories of Detroit, *Reaching for the Sun* is one of the more unusual films of its time. It is a film by William Wellman that somehow receives much less attention than his others. Its genesis is the Wessel Smitter novel *F. O. B. Detroit*, a socially significant book about the conflict of man against machines. W. L. River's screenplay pivots the action around one of those all-important little matters upon which lives often expand or go astray. In this case it is an outboard motor which a clam digging woodsman of Michigan craves in order to lighten his labors. It eventually stands as a symbol of what he regards as his freedom in the open wilds, where "everything reaches for the sun." Wellman astutely regarded Joel McCrea the right actor to play this resolute soul.

Russ Elliott (McCrea) reckons that the best way for him to get his outdooor motor, and thereby increase his clam digging business, is to go to Detroit and work in a car factory. He and his pal Benny Morgan (Eddie Bracken) do just that and Elliott soon has all the money he needs; but, he has also acquired a wife, Rita (Ellen Drew), who does not quite share his enthusiasm for the outboard motor. Once she becomes pregnant, she views the motor as a rival, one that will take her and her husband away from the city where she would rather live, and which she is convinced will provide a better home for their child.

With Ellen Drew.

After a lot of marital wrangling results in a separation, Elliott is badly hurt in a factory fight with a section boss (Albert Dekker). They fight on the giant factory machines, using large tools and chains as weapons. Visiting him in the hospital, Rita finally agrees that life in the country would be better for them - living in a cottage alongside a wood-fringed lake, listening to the purr of an outboard moter rather than the din of industrial life in the city. They take Benny with them but he soon leaves, preferring city noise to the quiet of the country, a quiet so intense he cannot sleep.

With Eddie Bracken.

McCrea plays the gentle but tough woodsman with just the right blend of broad humor, contrasting it with moments of dramatic intensity. The part fits, and once again it was a matter of working with a director in whom he had complete trust, William Wellman.

SULLIVAN'S TRAVELS

Paramount, 1941;
Produced by Paul Jones; Directed and written by Preston Sturges; Photographed by John F. Seitz; Music by Leo Shukin and Charles Bradshaw; 91 minutes.

Cast:
John L. Sullivan, Joel McCrea; *The Girl*, Veronica Lake; *Mr. Lebrand*, Robert Warrick; *Mr. Jones*, William Demarest; *Mr. Casalsis*, Franklin Pangborn; *Mr. Hadrian*, Porter Hall; *Mr. Valdelle*, Byron Foulger; *Secretary*, Margaret Hayes; *Butler*, Robert Greig; *Valet*, Eric Blore.

Enter Preston Sturges into the career of Joel Mc-Crea - a major entry. The two men were vastly different. Sturges was an eccentric of flamboyant style and McCrea was the opposite, yet there was a natural rapport between the two and a great liking, one for the other. They would make three films together, two hits and a miss. The first remains one of the wittiest and most knowing satires on Holly-wood, *Sullivan's Travels*. It came in the wake of Sturges' success with *The Lady Eve* (1941), and he would follow it with *The Palm Beach Story*, which would also star McCrea, and two bizarre comedies with Eddie Bracken, *The Miracle of Morgan's Creek* (1944), and *Hail to the Conquering Hero* (1944). These were the peak of the Sturges Hollywood career.

Born into a wealthy family, he had been a successful screen writer at Paramount all through the Thirties. In 1940, he finally persuaded the studio to let him direct one of his own stories, *The Great McGinty*. Part of the agreement was that the screenplay would cost virtually nothing. Four years later he declined Paramount's offer of a one million dollar contract, preferring to go his own way as an independant, a decision that unfortunately slowly lead downhill.

Sullivan's Travels pokes fun at the motion picture business but not in a cruel way. Sturges had sting in his barbs but he was by nature, a compassionate man. His John L. Sullivan (McCrea) is a successful movie director looking to do a film of social significance, something beyond mere entertainment. When first seen, he is discussing his view in a screening room with studio executives Labrand (Robert Warwick) and Hadrian (Porter Hall). He wants to make a picture called *Brother, Where Art Thou?*, in which he can point up the inequities between capitalism and labor. Both executives respond with total disinterest and suggest instead a musical,

With Veronica Lake.

With Eric Blore.

to which Sullivan angrily responds, "How can you talk about musicals at a time like this, with the world committing suicide...with grim death gargling at you from every corner...?" Replies Hadrian, "Maybe they'd like to forget that."

Sullivan gives up trying to convince them and instead decides to take a close look at real life, to go out among the common people and see what reality is all about. So he goes to the studio' costume department to get decked out as a hobo, and in this grubby attire, he has his chauffeur drop him off in a run-down area of the city without any money. What happens to him turns out to be much worse than anything he had imagined.

Sullivan meets a young woman (Veronica Lake), a would-be movie actress down on her luck. Together they travel around, hopping on freight trains, sleeping in missions and scavenging for food. Whenever he talks grandly about the nobility of film as a great educational force she yawns. His butler (Robert Greig) does more than yawn, he tells Sullivan in so many words that poverty is a vile thing, a plague to be stayed away from, even for the purposes of study.

Sullivan is arrested as a vagrant and shipped off to a prison farm where he is assigned to a chain gang. His most important lesson as a film maker comes at the prison farm. He causes such an uproar that he gets his photo in the newspapers, enabling his concerned studio to locate him. One evening he observes how a cartoon affects the audience, how its humor brings a temporary relief from their despair. With that in mind, he is released after being identified by the studio. Once back at the studio, Sullivan meets with his executives who have publicized his adventures and are now interested in having him do a film about social values and problems. But Sullivan, a man with new awareness, protests. He knows his job is to entertain. "There's a lot to be said for making people laugh. Did you know that's all some people have? It isn't much, but it's better than nothing in this cockeyed caravan."

Sturges' Sullivan is obviously somewhat autobiographical, although with the irony that Sturges entertained while also managing to make trenchant comments on the human condition and some of the more bizarre facets of the American way of life. For Joel McCrea, it was a major film in his career and the first time he had had a script tailored for him. Sturges made more films with McCrea than any other leading man and it is possible that he saw McCrea as a kind of screen image of himself. He had admired McCrea for a long time and told him

years previously that he would use him if ever he became a director.

For Sturges, McCrea personified the slightly comic side of American male assuredness, the vulnerable chink in its armor, as in the case of Sullivan who sallies forth with innocence, only to suffer humiliations he never dreamed of. The quiet, stalwart McCrea image was precisely what Sturges needed for this film, and he put McCrea at ease by telling him just that. "He came to me with the script and said it was for me. I knew he could get Fonda, or Jimmy Stewart or Cary Grant but he said he wanted me, and that gave me the confidence to try different things and live up to what he expected of me. He wrote his scripts with specific actors in mind."

In order to do *Sullivan's Travels* McCrea turned down Cecil B. DeMille's offer to star in *Reap the Wild Wind*, the part that later went to John Wayne. DeMille was amazed that McCrea would make this deci-sion and advised him against it, saying that although Sturges was a brilliant writer the film would probably be forgotten. McCrea's decision was based on the fact that Sturges *was* a brilliant writer. "In doing a picture that's what I based my opinions on - not what they were going to pay me, but the script, especially when someone tells you they've written it with you in mind, and if the writer also happens to be the director, and if he is as articulate as Sturges."

Considering the bizzarre nature of Sturges' films and his own eccentricities, it might be assumed that he was not very practical in his work methods. This was not the case. According to McCrea, Sturges seldom shot more than three takes, "He wasted less time and less film than anyone, except maybe Hitchcock." The long opening scene in *Sullivan's Travels*, in which the director argues with the studio executives was scheduled for a two-day shoot. Instead it was done in one morning, with the main section done on the first take, something that became a conversation piece around Paramount for some while. Apparently no director before then had ever put ten minutes of material "in one can" with a couple of hours of work. Sturges liked to get his long, dialogue sequences done in continuous takes and leave his time for the more quirky shorter bits.

THE GREAT MAN'S LADY

Paramount, 1942;
Produced and directed by William Wellman; Written by Adela Rogers St. John and Sean Owen, based on the story by Vina Delmar; Photographed by William C. Mellor; Music by Victor Young; 90 minutes.

Cast:
Hannah Sempler, Barbara Stanwyck; *Ethan Hoyt*, Joel McCrea; *Steely Edwards*, Brian Donlevy; *Girl Biographer*, Katharine Stevens; *Mr. Sempler*, Thurston Hall; *Mr. Cadwallader*, Lloyd Corrigan; *Delilah*, Etta McDaniel; *Senator Knobs*, Frank M. Thomas; *Mandy*, Lillian Yarbo; *Bettina*, Helen Lynd; *Persis*, Mary Treen; *City Editor*, Lucien Littlefield; *Senator Grant*, John Hamilton.

The Great Man's Lady is much more about the lady than the great man, giving Barbara Stanwyck one of the highlights of her lengthy career. She portrays a frontier woman who ages to 109, in a story that begins when the character she plays is in her late teens. When the picture was being planned by producer-director William Wellman, there was no doubt which actor would play the great man, western idealist Ethan Hoyt. The part was virtually tailored for Joel McCrea.

The film expands the James M. Barrie thesis, propounded in his play *What Every Woman Knows*, that behind every great man there is a great woman pushing him on to success. As the film opens Hannah Sempler (Stanwyck) is being interviewed by a young woman (Katherine Stevens) who is writing a biography of Ethan Hoyt. She arrives to see Hannah on the day a statue of Hoyt is being unveiled in the public square of Hoyt City. Many have tried unsuccessfully to get Hannah to tell the story of her association with the long since deceased Hoyt; now she decides to reveal it to this sincere young writer. She tells of being the product of a stuffy Philadelphia family, of meeting Hoyt when she was only sixteen, galloping off on horseback to marry him in a heavy prairie rainstorm, living on the primitive frontier with him, shooting game, fighting with him, and tragically losing her two children in a flood. Hannah also tells of confronting a gambler (Brian Donlevy) with a revolver in a saloon and getting back everything her husband has lost.

Hannah is a complex woman, who downplays her own interests in favor of her husband, and often acts tougher than she really is. She contrives to help his career but effaces herself so that Hoyt may have

With Barbara Stanwyck.

With Stanwyck and Lloyd Corrigan.

With Brian Donlevy.

the success for which she believes he was intended. Eventually it costs her her marriage, as she virtually provoked a separation in order to give Hoyt the freedom he needs to create businesses and take part in politics. She lives many more years after the divorce, leaving people in her old age wondering if she ever did know the great man.

The film met with only moderate success when released in the Spring of 1942. Critics praised Stanwyck for the skill and the range of her performance but the public, possibly expecting a rip, roaring western, were disappointed to find it the story of a courageous woman who had sacrificed herself to help a man and lost not only him but her children. The more knowledgeable critics complimented Wally Westmore for his superb make-up for the aged lady and some noted the fine work of Brian Donlevy, playing the gambler whose feelings for Hannah go unrewarded. McCrea also won a few points with a few critics who felt it was among his best work, even though he appears in only about half of the film. But he makes no bones about whose film it is when he says, "Stanwyck should have gotten an award for this film - if ever anyone ever deserved it."

THE PALM BEACH STORY

Paramount, 1942;
Produced by Paul Jones; Directed and written by Preston Sturges; Photographed by Victor Milner; Music by Victor Young; 88 minutes.

Cast:
Gerry Jeffers, Claudette Colbert; *Tom Jeffers*, Joel McCrea; *Princess*, Mary Astor; *John D. Hackensacker, III*, Rudy Vallee; *Apartment Manager*, Franklin Pangborn; *The*

Weinie King, Robert Dudley; *Toto*, Sig Arno; *and the members of the Ale and Quail Club*: William Demarest, Robert Warrick, Arthur Stuart Hill, Torben Meyer, Jimmy Conlin, Vic Potel, Jack Norton, Robert Greig, Roscoe Ates, Dewey Robinson, Chester Conklin and Sheldon Jett

After spoofing Hollywood with *Sullivan's Travels*, Preston Sturges turned his piquant humor on an even wider target - the foibles of the American rich. *The Palm Beach Story* does it in a slightly perverse, Sturgean way by first focusing on the predicament of not having money. Its protagonists are a handsome married couple, Tom and Gerry Heffers (McCrea and Claudette Colbert), who are still deeply in love after five years of marriage but desperate for lack of funds. He is an inventor unable to interest backers in his revolutionary ideas. His wife decides that the only way she can help him is to divorce him, land a wealthy husband and then subsideize him.

As Tom and Gerry are about to give up their apartment, a strange elf-like little old man (Robert Dudley) wanders in to take a look at it, announcing that he is America's Wienie King. This half-deaf eccentric is so unconcerned about money that he carries wads of bills in his pockets, and when he hears of Gerry's troubles he shoves money into her hands. With this she decides to take a train to Palm Beach and look for the wealthy husband-to-be.

With Claudette Colbert.

With Rudy Vallee, Mary Astor, and Claudette Colbert.

The train ride turns out to be quite an experience. She enters into the boisterous company of a wild group who call themselves The Ale and Quail Club. These wealthy buffoons, off on a hunting spree, are millionaires who think nothing of firing off their guns inside the train. To get rid of them, the conductors unhitch the club car and leave it on a siding. Gerry, still in the club car and out of cash, easily ingratiates herself into the affections of mild-mannered John D. Hackensacker, III (Rudy Valee). She accepts an invitation to be his house guest, which includes a cruise on his yacht.

Gerry now comes into contact with John's man-hungry sister (Mary Astor), known as the Princess because she was once married to a Prince. Tom, who had never agreed to his wife's wild plan, arrives on the scene, angry that Gerry had left without his consent and intent on taking her home. But Gerry had further tricks up her sleeve. She persuades Tom to pose as her brother because she believes she can get from the amorous Hackensacker the capital to finance Tom's plans for a downtown airport. Hackensacker proposes marriage and the Princess decides that Tom will be the next husband on her roster. The morass of complications subsides when Gerry and Tom reveal their true relationship, adding - and thereby soving the problem - that they both have identical twins. *The Palm Beach Story* reaches a happy ending with the double weddings of Hackensacker and Gerry's sister, and The Princess with Tom's brother.

Sturges clearly enjoyed needling the superwealthy and their dizzy social lives - actually the environment in which he had been born - but he always did it without being malicious. He was a satirist with a fondness for human kind, as well as a writer-director with a keen eye for casting. The choice of Claudette Colbert was obvious in view of her expertise in romantic comedies, but Sturges surprised the industry by seeing something in Rudy Vallee no one else had spotted. The veteran crooner was always a little pompous of manner and self assured to the point of being smug, but in allowing Sturges to play up those traits, Vallee's career was given a new twist. From then on Vallee was often John D. Hackensacker, III, culminating in his "Grand Old Ivy" tycoon in *How to Succeed in Business Without Really Trying.*

It was Preston Sturges who saw something in the Joel McCrea screen persona that no one else had apparently noted, perhaps even McCrea himself - humor. By 1941, the McCrea image was fairly well set, that of the solid American male, cool and calm, a fundamental sanity, and not very funny. Sturges realized that there was a counterpoint to that image, in musical terms, the occasional striking of a minor note in a major scale. Hence, the puzzlement of the McCrea characters in finding themselves in situations they cannot quite grasp - John L. Sullivan coming up against the reality of poverty and Tom Jeffers trying to figure out the wacky people in *The Palm Beach Story*, wis wife included.

What Sturges had done with Henry Fonda in *The Lady Eve* (1941) was to turn an essentially dramatic actor into a light comedian. What he did with McCrea was much the same, tilting the somewhat self-righteous, innocent guise of the uncompromising hero in the direction of implied absurdity. And under Sturges' tutelage McCrea became adept at something he had never tackled before - extended, snappy dialogue.

THE MORE THE MERRIER

Columbia, 1943;
Produced and directed by George Stevens; Written by Robert Russell, Frank Ross, Richard Flournoy and Lewis R. Foster; Photographed by Ted Tetzlaff; Music by Leigh Harline; 104 minutes.

Cast:
Connie Milligan, Jean Arthur; *Joe Carter*, Joel McCrea; *Benjamin Dingle*, Charles Coburn; *Charles J. Pendergast*, Richard Gaines; *Evans*, Bruce Bennett; *Pike*, Frank Sully; *Senator Noonan*, Clyde Fillmore; *Morton Rodakiewiez*, Stanley Clements; *Harding*, Don Douglas; *Miss Dalton*, Ann Savage; *Waiter*, Grady Sutton.

For contemporary audiences to appreciate the basis of the humor in *The More the Merrier* requires some understanding of Washington, D. C. during the war years. Prior to the war the city was fairly small in its work community; with the war it became packed with military, diplomatic and enlarged government bodies, causing an acute housing problem. Quick, sly and furtive dealings often overcame rank and money in finding a place to live. Producer-director George Stevens astutely sized this up for its comic possibilities, and it is because of Steven's skill and sly sense of humor that *The More the Merrier* remains a classic American comdey, as well as one of the film's by which Joel McCrea is most remembered. Not surprisingly, it was also one of his own favorites.

In less talented hands the film might not have worked because the basis of the humor lies in the interplay between the three main characters - a government secretary, Connie Milligan (Jean Arthur), an Army Air Corps technician, Joe Carter (McCrea), on assignment in Washington in civilian clothes, and Benjamin Dingle (Charles Coburn), who describes himself as a retired millionaire but who also has a secret government assignment. Against her will, Connie agrees to rent half of her apartment to Dingle, who merely dismisses the other possible renters. His motto is, "Damn the torpedoes! Full speed ahead!" That attitude prevails when Dingle assesses the plight of Carter, who is wandering around carrying an airplane propeller and looking for somewhere to stay. So Dingle rents him half of his half of the apartment.

With Charles Coburn and three unidentified beauties.

With Jean Arthur.

With Arthur and Coburn

With director George Stevens.

Connie tries to run the crowded apartment along efficient lines and issues written instructions for timings of movements. These confuse the elderly Dingle, who manages to lock himself out, make his bed with his trousers in it and pour coffee in the bath tub while struggling to dress. Dingle is also of a mind to play Cupid, believing that Carter would be a better match for Connie than the pompous government official, Charles J. Pendergast (Richard Gaines) to whom she is engaged. But Dingle oversteps the mark when he reads Connie's diary, resulting in her asking Dingle to leave and to take Carter with him. The old fellow goes but not Carter, who has now become fond of Connie despite her avowed lack of interest.

Dingle finds other accomodations, but the more he sees of the fussy Pendergast, the more he is determined to see that Carter gets Connie. Carter's situation takes a turn for the worse when the FBI comes to arrest him; shortly before he had warded off a pesky young boy by claiming to be a Japanese spy, with the boy making a report to the FBI. Pendergast arrives on the scene and is more shocked to find that Connie has been sharing accomodations with Carter than Carter's being arrested as a spy. Deliberately making the situation seem worse, Dingle claims never to have stayed with Connie.

A newspaper report about Pendergast's fiancee sharing her apartment with a possible spy moves the nervous official to get the charges dropped. He then offers the suggestion that Connie and Carter get married, followed by an annullment. Connie now sees Pendergast as the cold-hearted careerist he is and dismisses him from her life. Then to spite him she goes ahead with the marriage, after which she and Carter return to the apartment not knowing how it is they feel about each other. Dingle slyly lifts their depression and prods them into realizing they are in love. With that scheme a success he yells, "Damn the torpedoes! Full steam ahead!"

The More the Merrier was nominated for an Academy Award as Best Film of 1942, but it lost to *Casablanca*. Jean Arthur was nominated as Best Actress, but lost to Jennifer Jones in *The Song of Bernadette*. George Stevens was nominated for Best Director, but lost to Michael Curtiz for *Casablanca*. Charles Coburn did receive an Oscar as best Supporting Actor as the wily old Dingle.

The most memorable scene in the film is the one in which McCrea and Arthur sit on the front steps of her apartment and talk. But what they talk about has no bearing upon their physical actions. He keeps touching her, her hand, arm, face, back and she fields and parries the touches while telling him about Pendergast and his job. He pretends to listen and voice little comments, none of which have anything to do with his leaning over to kiss her ear or stroking her back. It is a quietly erotic scene, beautifully handled by expert players and directed by Stevens, who was a master at timing and improvisation. He got the idea for the scene from watching McCrea flirt with Arthur, something both he and McCrea deliberately did in order to build up her confidence.

Jean Arthur was never very secure about acting and needed a great deal of coaxing and flattering and beguiling. Long unhappy working for Columbia's shrewd but crude boss, Harry Cohn, Arthur was already thinking about getting out of the business, although she would make three more films before arriving at that decision in 1948. However, it would be George Stevens who would manage to coax her out of retirement five years later to co-star in *Shane*.

McCrea came into the film because both Stevens and Arthur wanted him. Stevens sent her out to McCrea's ranch with a few pages of the script to try to get his interest. McCrea, who had known Arthur since the days when they were both extras, opted for doing *The More the Merrier* both because of Arthur's pleas and upon being told that Stevens had turned down Cary Grant and Robert Montgomery for the role. With that McCrea went to see Cohn, feigned slight interest and allowed Cohn to work himself up into an angry insistence that McCrea had to do the picture.

Stevens, whom McCrea described as one of his favorite directors and "a very sensitive, meticulous worker - one of the best directors our industry ever had," wanted McCrea for *Shane*, for the role eventually played by Van Heflin. As he had so many times by now, McCrea talked himself out of the job. "I didn't want to do it. I loved working with George and I would have worked for nothing but it was Alan Ladd's picture. Alan and I were good friends and I don't think it would have helped him if I'd been in the film. Besides, as I told George, I wasn't ready to play a secondary role, so they got Van Heflin and he was great. He was better in it than I would have been. But I loved the picture, an excellent, wonderful picture."

BUFFALO BILL

20th Century-Fox, 1944;
Produced by Harry Sherman; Directed by William Wellman; Written by Aeneas MacKenzie, Clements Ripley and Cecil Kramer, based on a story by Frank Winch; Photographed in Technicolor by Leon Shamroy; Music by David Buttolph; 90 minutes.

Cast:
Buffalo Bill, Joel McCrea; *Louise*, Maureen O'Hara; *Dawn Starlight*, Linda Darnell; *Ned Buntline*, Thomas Mitchell; *Sergeant Chips*, Edgar Buchanan; *Yellow Hand*, Anthony Quinn; *Senator Frederici*, Moroni Olsen; *Murdo Carvell*, Frank Fenton; *General Blazier*, Matt Briggs; *Mr.*

Vandervere, George Lessey; *Sherman*, Frank Orth; *Trooper Clancy*, George Chandler; *Crazy Horse*, Chief Thundercloud; *Theodore Roosevelt*, Sidney Blackmer.

William Frederick Cody (1846-1917) was not a man likely to be overlooked by the motion picture industry. He had been a Pony Express rider and a Union Army scout while a teenager, and following the Civil War he was a guide for western expeditions and a supplyer of buffalo meat to the army and the railroads. Cody took part in the campaigns against the warring Indians but afterwards took a stand on their behalf when he felt they had been unfairly treated. However, his real fame came when he met journalist Ned Buntline, who dubbed Cody 'Buffalo Bill' and filled magazines and dime novels with colorfully exaggerated accounts of Cody's adventures. A celebrated figure by the birth of the movies, Cody made appearances in several and when Universal Studios opened in 1915 he was the guest of honor. That he should be portrayed in the movies was inevitable. He was first played by Art Acord in *In the Days of Buffalo Bill* in 1923, and afterwards turned up as a figure in such epics as *The Iron Horse* (1924), *The Pony Express* (1925), *The Plainsman* (1937), and in any number of B westerns. However, it was not until 1944 that a major film was made about Cody, with Joel McCrea the actor selected to play him.

Buffalo Bill was the brainchild of producer Harry Sherman, the man who brought Hopalong Cassidy to the screen and who also made many admirable westerns. 20th Century Fox accepted his concept

With Robert Idomans (the policeman).

With Thomas Mitchell.

92

and three scenarists finally came up with a script that met with their approval. They assigned William Wellman to direct, but after reading the script he begged off. Fox insisted, and reminded him that in order to make the *film noir* western *The Ox-Bow Incident* (1943), he had agreed to direct any film they next gave him. He was stuck. What Wellman objected to was the blandly heroic characterization of Cody, the conventional glorification, the commercialization of the West, for which Hollywood itself was the primary villain. It was not until many years later that the movies took a more realistic and often cynical look at American historical figures, with Paul Newman's version of a less agreeable Cody in *Buffalo Bill and the Indians* (1976), being a prime example.

However, in 1944 the accent was on the grandly heroic and the noble, and that was how McCrea played Cody. The film opens with accounts of Cody's work as a meat contractor, cutting out buffalo from the vast herds, while at the same time expressing concern for excessive slaughtering of the Indians' main source of food and clothing. He rescues a stage coach from Indian attack and finds one of the passengers to be a lovely lady, Louise (Maureen O'Hara), traveling with her senator father (Moroni Olsen) and several other government officials assessing the western situation. Cody and Louise fall in love and get married, over the objections of her parents and to the sadness of an Indian schoolteacher (Linda Darnell), who has long loved Cody.

Cody is hired as a guide and adviser by the army in its campaign against warring Indians led by the Cheyenne Chief Yellow Hand (Anthony Quinn). In the epic battle of War Bonnet Gorge Cody personally challenges the Chief and kills him in hand-to-hand combat. For his part in the campaign Cody is awarded the Congressional Medal of Honor.

His success with the army causes Cody to lose his wife. When he decides to go on the campaign against her wishes, leaving her with their infant son, Louise returns to her family home in Washington. Cody later comes to the capital. At first, he is lauded for his exploits, but then he is shunted aside as he makes a nuisance of himself talking about Indian rights and the deprivations of business interests. His lack of success is made the more tragic when he visits Louise and finds his son dying of diphtheria.

With no money Cody becomes a virtual derelict, the only employment he can find is as an attraction in a carnival show. It is there that the shrewd Ned Buntline (Thomas Mitchell) spots him and sees the potential. Cody agrees to let Buntline write about him, with the successful yarns leading to Cody being

With Lester Dorr and Edgar Buchanan.

93

offered his own Wild West Show. With Louise reunited with him after finding him in the carnival, he travels America and the world and becomes the beloved 'Buffalo Bill.'

As a film *Buffalo Bill* is far too sentimantal, and oddly unexciting, except for the admirably staged battle sequence with the Indians. Joel McCrea conveys the nobility but, as written, the role is somewhat dull. He looks splendid, especially in the final sequences as the bearded Cody, gracefully riding around the arena as hordes of young boy cheer him. But the concept is stilted, and William Wellman practically disowned the film. The easiest way to rile the feisty director was to mention *Buffalo Bill*.

THE GREAT MOMENT

Paramount, 1944;
Directed and written by Preston Sturges, based on the book *Triumph Over Pain* by René Fulop-Miller; Photographed by Victor Milner; Music by Victor Young; 83 minutes.

Cast:
W. T. G. Morton, Joel McCrea; *Mrs. Morton*, Betty Field; *Professor Warren*, Harry Carey; *Eben Frost*, William Demarest; *Horace Wells*, Louis Jean Heydt; *Dr. Jackson*, Julius Tannen; *Medical Society VP*, Edwin Maxwell; *President Pierce*, Porter Hall; *Dr. Heywood*, Franklin Pangborn; *Homer Quinby*, Grady Sutton; *Betty Morton*, Donivee Lee; *Judge Shipman*, Harry Hayden; *Dr. Dahlmeyer*, Torben Meyer.

Of the eight films Preston Sturges made at Paramount, the only flop was *The Great Moment*, the third of his films with Joel McCrea. It was also the only one that was not an original screenplay. Instead, it was a Sturges script based on a book, a biography of Boston dentist, W.T.G. Morton, who pioneered the use of ether as an anaesthetic in the late Nineteenth century. Telling this story on the screen had long been a passion for Sturges, albeit a curious one, and one which the studio would never have allowed him to tackle had it not been for his recent successes. It was difficult to even arrive at a title. The title of the book by René Fulop-Miller, *Triumph Over Pain*, was immediately rejected by Paramount, and Sturges' suggested *Great Without Glory* met with no enthusiasm. The vague *The Great Moment* left everyone wondering what it was all about.

The film was completed in June of 1942, but not released for two years. Paramount was hoping that Sturges' interim success with *The Miracle of Morgan's Creek* and *Hail the Conquering Hero*, along with McCrea's exposure in *The More the Merrier* and *Buffalo Bill* might create sufficient public interest to return their investment. None of this helped the orphan film, which went through so much editing that in the end only Sturges himself knew what he originally had in mind. What emerged was a strange mixture of poignancy and tragedy, laced with bits of slapstick comedy and shards of satire. But for all that *The Great Moment* is a film with many great moments and a performance by McCrea that is possibly his most complex and interesting.

The story of Dr. Morton is a sad one. After discovering ether as an anaestetic, he was ridiculed. Then after its acceptance, he gave away the secret and ended up being ruined and driven into despair by the profession which had benefitted by his work. He was a difficult man. In trying to hype the public interest Paramount invented exciting wordage for their ads, "Only the Woman he loved believed in him. . . and sometimes even she had her doubts." As written by Sturges and played by the excellent Betty Field, Mrs. Lizzie Morton had reasons for her doubts.

The film begins with a flashback as Eben Frost (William Demarest), the first man to receive Morton's treatment, redeems a citation from a pawnshop and brings it to Lizzie. It is a medal Morton had received from the French government, marking

With William Demarest.

94

With Betty Field.

his contributions to mankind with his humanitarian concern for the relieving of pain in medical operations. Lizzie is moved to reminisce about the sad last years of his life, the years of frustration and neglect. The film then goes into another flashback, recalling Morton's early years as a dentist and his struggles to help his patients in their sufferings with pain. He discovers the properties of ether when a fire boils the chemical by accident, causing him to pass out. He then realizes the efficacy of the vapor, but his wife assumes he has been drinking when she finds him lying on the floor. She does not understand his explanation or his attempt to test out his new theories on their dog.

Eben Frost reacts violently after subjecting himself to the first experiment, jumping out the window and attacking people, causing Morton to realize he had overdone the dose. But Frost soon becomes Morton's biggest booster, spending the rest of his life recalling, "It was the evening of September 30th, I was in excruciating pain. . ." The discovery of ether narcosis brings Morton a brief period of fame and fortune, but he is a poor businessman and much too soft hearted. He gives away the secret of the anaesthetic in order to save an

impoverished girl the agony of pain she would otherwise suffer in a surgical operation. His breakthrough is claimed by others, he is discredited and gradually drifts into despair, bitterly thinking back on the one "great moment" when he decided to sacrifice himself in order to help the girl.

The mixture of tragedy and comedy was more than even a genius like Preston Sturges could bring off. However, *The Great Moment* is an interesting film study, and a revelation of how good an actor McCrea could be, given the right material and direction. His performance is the best thing about the film. Sturges obviously knew he had picked the right actor to portray doggedness. McCrea never at any time looked like a man who could be pushed around, and no actor in the movies ever better conveyed an air of quirky dignity, which is precisely the characteristic Sturges needed for his concept of Dr. W.T.G. Morton. Sturges also tapped in McCrea something else nobody had previously spotted—a certain quiet anger hovering beneath that calm, dignified stance. Nowhere in the McCrea career is it more in evidence than in *The Great Moment*.

While they were working on *Sullivan's Travels*,

Sturges told McCrea that he would use him in half a dozen pictures, but with Sturges leaving Paramount and McCrea following other committments, they were never able to get together again. And with the exceptions of his two other favorite directors, George Stevens and Gregory La Cava, no other director got from McCrea performances like those of Sturges. While McCrea was mostly of sane demeanor in his films, it is only in the three with Sturges that he leaned in the direction of being a little manic, or as Sturges would have said, "nutty." This was possible only because of the confidence the director was able to give to the actor, and the warm regard the two had for each other. While *The Lady Eve* is regarded by many as the greatest Sturges comedy, with a brilliantly comic performance by Henry Fonda, McCrea says, "He never used Fonda again, and he's a better actor than I am. But Fonda wasn't in love with Sturges and I was."

THE UNSEEN

Paramount, 1945;
Produced by John Houseman; Directed by Lewis Allen;

With Gail Russell and Herbert Marshall.

Written by Hagar Wilde and Raymond Chandler, based on the novel *Her Heart in Her Throat* by Ethel Lina White; Photographed by John F. Seitz; Music by Ernst Toch; 80 minutes.

Cast:
David Fielding, Joel McCrea; *Elizabeth Howard*, Gail Russell; *Dr. Charles Evans*, Herbert Marshall; *Maxine*, Phyllis Brooks; *Marian Typarth*, Isobel Elsom; *Jaspar Goodwin*, Norman Lloyd; *Chester*, Mikhail Rasumny; *Mrs. Norris*, Elizabeth Risdon; *Sullivan*, Tom Tully; *Ellen Fielding*, Nona Griffith; *Bainaby Fielding*, Richard Lyon.

Paramount enjoyed a hit with its chilling and stylish ghost story *The Uninvited* in 1944 and tried to follow the success a year later with *The Unseen*, employing the same British director, Lewis Allen, and the same leading lady, the ethereal and fragile beauty, Gail Russell. The film failed to measure up to the former one but still provided some scary sequences, while also providing Joel McCrea with one of the strangest roles in his career and his only work in a frightening picture. The role is of a bitter, brooding widower, trying to bring up his two children in a house permeated with gloom, some caused by a former governess and all of it upsetting to the new governess. The screenplay, for which Raymond Chandler was a contributor, was based

on a novel by Ethel Lina White, but her inspiration could have been nothing other than Henry James' *The Turn of a Screw*.

David Fielding (McCrea), surly and withdrawn since the death under suspicious circumstances of his wife, hires the lovely, young Elizabeth Howard (Russell) to take care of his two children, winsome Ellen (Nona Griffith), who keeps a picture of a corpse pasted in her scrapbook but refuses to tell why, and Bainaby (Richard Lyon), who is sullen and uncommunicative. The house in which they live is next to another that has been boarded up for twelve years, following the death of its owner. Elizabeth finds that the sinister influence of the previous governess dominates the children, particularly the boy. He remembers the governess with affection and plays over and over a record she gave him. He keeps the faucet running at night in order to stay awake, and he insists that the house next door is inhabited. In fact, he claims that this mysterious person pays him money to perform certain services. When two murders take place in the area it becomes apparent that the boy's secret is a dangerous one.

With Herbert Marshall.

Elizabeth is moved to find out what is really going on, and comes close to being murdered as a result. She enters the old house next door and finds her way along dark, musty corridors into the cellar. Fielding slowly emerges from his depression and grows to love the young lady who shows so much concern for the welfare of his children. Together they solve the mystery of the house and the identity of the murderer. Who is he or she? Let those who have not seen *The Unseen* find out for themselves.

In reviewing the film the *Hollywood Reporter* said that McCrea "offers a brilliant interpretation of the moody father who finally awakens." Other re-

viewers complimented him and assumed he would now broaden his dramatic scope. McCrea, however, was about to do the opposite. With only one exception the remainder of his career as a film actor would be in westerns.

THE VIRGINIAN

Paramount, 1946;
Produced by Paul Jones; Directed by Stuart Gillmore;
Written by Frances Goodrich and Albert Hackett,

With Sonny Tufts.

With Brian Donlevy and Tufts. "...when you call me that, smile."

adapted from the 1929 screenplay by Howard Estabrook of the play by Owen Wister and Kirk La Shelle, based on Wister's novel; Photographed in Technicolor by Harry Hallenberger; Music by Daniele Amfitheatrof; 90 minutes.

Cast:
The Virginian, Joel McCrea; *Trampas*, Brian Donlevy; *Steve*, Sonny Tufts; *Molly*, Barbara Britton; *Mrs. Taylor*, Fay Bainter; *Nebraska*, Tom Tully; *Mr. Taylor*, Henry O'Neill; *Sam Bennett*, Bill Edwards; *Honey Wiggan*, William Frawley; *Shorty*, Paul Guilfoyle; *Pete*, Marc Lawrence; *Baldy*, Vince Barnett.

The most time honored western story is probably that of *The Virginian*, which began its life as a novel by Owen Wister and was adapted into a stage play by the author and Kirk La Shelle. The play starred an actor well known for his Shakespearean performances, William S. Hart. That was in 1907, and his success in that play was one of the factors leading to Hart becoming a legendary figure in film westerns. However, Hart never played the role on the screen. The first film version in 1914 starred Dustin Farnum, a popular movie cowboy of the period, and

was directed for Paramount by Cecil B. DeMille. It was filmed again in 1923 with Kenneth Harlan, and once more in 1929 with Gary Cooper, his first film completely in sound. It was also Cooper's first major success and triggered a spectacular career. In 1946, it occurred to Paramount producer Paul Jones, who had produced the Preston Sturges movies, to drag the story out again and use Joel McCrea as the quiet, stalwart cowboy who, when called a dirty name by the villain in a saloon, advises, "When you call me that, smile."

The plot of the McCrea version is largely that of the original. The Virginian—he is known to everybody only by that name—is the foreman of a large cattle ranch, near the town of Medicine Bow, Wyoming. Rustling is taking place in the area and the Virginian suspects that the man behind it is Trampas (Brian Donlevy), a gambler who runs a saloon. He is the one who smiles when the Virginian sticks a gun in his midriff in response to the insult. The Virginian is elected by the local ranchers to form a posse to seek out the rustlers. This bothers Molly (Barbara Britton), a refined school teacher from Vermont, who

With Tufts, Barbara Britton, and Bill Edwards.

has fallen in love with the Virginian and does not want to see him involved in anything dangerous.

The Virginian and his men capture three rustlers, with an immediate decision to hang them. This is traumatic for the Virginian because one of them is Steve (Sonny Tufts), a happy-go-lucky cowhand who is the Virginian's best friend. Steve goes to his death telling his friend that he understands but not telling him, as the Virginian suspects, that Trampas is the man for whom he has been doing the rustling. Having had to hang Steve causes the Virginian to be resolute in tracking Trampas, even though it brings him into open conflict with Molly. But when the Virginian is badly wounded while going after the rustlers it is Molly who nurses him back to health. Trampas, knowing he has to get rid of the Virginian in order to continue, challenges him in the streets of Medicine Bow, and in the subsequent shoot-out, loses his life.

The Virginian, beautifully filmed in Technicolor by Harry Hallenberger, is a well produced western but one lacking much flare. In the minds of western buffs it did not replace the Gary Cooper version, although a better reason for the mild response was that, by 1946, the plot had become such a cliche that no amount of production values could make it seem credible. A new attitude in the making of westerns was now needed, and Joel McCrea would be very much involved in determining what that attitude would be.

RAMROD

United Artists, 1947;
Produced by Harry Sherman; Directed by Andre de Toth; Written by Jack Moffitt, Graham Baker and Cecile Kramer, based on the novel by Luke Short; Photographed by Russell Harlan; Music by Adolph Deutsch; 94 minutes.

Cast:
Dave Nash, Joel McCrea; *Connie Dickason*, Veronica Lake; *Walt Shipley*, Ian McDonald; *Ben Dickason*, Wesley Ruggles; *Frank Ivy*, Preston Foster; *Rose*, Arleen Whelan; *Red Cates*, Lloyd Bridges; *Bill Schell*, Don De Fore; *Sheriff Jim Crow*, Donald Crisp.

Concepts in films began to change in the years following the second World War. The escapism that had been a profitable factor during the war years was no longer in vogue in what now seemed like a much less innocent America. Actors, writers and directors returning from war service had a different, more realistic attitude toward the making of movies. That attitude spilled over into westerns, with *Ramrod* being a case in point. The veteran producer, Harry Sherman, shared the view that a western with the right scripting and direction could play to an adult audience, as well as the juvenile one for which the majority of westerns had previously been made.

Sherman formed a new company, Enterprise, and for its first production he bought the rights to

With Don DeFore.

With Veronica Lake, Robert Wood, and Charlie Ruggles.

Ramrod, a novel by Luke Short, whose own experiences in the West, plus his enthusiasm for western history, gave his stories a wider range than the usual Wild West yarn. Short's stories were skillfully plotted, often violent and tended toward the darker side of human nature. To direct *Ramrod* Sherman picked the Hungarian-born Andre de Toth, just back from the war and a man with a tough, dramatic style. In Joel McCrea, the producer and the director found a willing ally in this more adult and sophisticated approach to western film.

In *Ramrod*, McCrea is Dave Nash, a cowhand who has been going through a bad period of drinking, brought on by the loss of his wife and child. Jim Crow (Donald Crisp), the veteran local sheriff is sympathetic to Nash and gets him a job as the foreman of a ranch owned by Connie Dickason (Veronica Lake), whose father (Wesley Ruggles) is in league with powerful rancher Frank Ivy (Preston Foster). Ivy wants to dominate the area but fails in winning the heart of Connie, who defies her father by running her ranch as she wants and not selling it to Ivy. Nash manages to round up enough cowboys to work the ranch, including his old friend Bill Schell (Don De Fore), who has a reputation for lawlessness.

Ivy's men attack and burn Connie's ranch, so Nash takes over one of Ivy's ranch stations. In trying to get it back Ivy savagely beats one of Connie's men, who later dies. To make Ivy look bad Connie entices Schell to stampede her herd at night and drive the cattle over a cliff but to tell no one about it. When

Sheriff Crow comes to arrest Ivy he is gunned down. Nash tracks one of Ivy's men and learns that Ivy is the culprit, but while tracking another one Nash is wounded. He manages to get back to town, where he is nursed by Rose (Arleen Whelan), a dressmaker who has long been in love with him.

To get Nash away from Ivy and his men, Schell takes him to a cave in the mountains, but Connie, in love with Nash, follows them. She in turn is tracked

With Preston Foster.

by Ivy. Schell sends the semi-conscious Nash, his left arm and shoulder tightly bandaged, off with Connie while he leads Ivy and his men astray. He holds them off on a rugged hillside until night, when Ivy creeps up and fires a shotgun into Schell's back.

A few days later the recovering Nash finds out about Connie's duplicity, which resulted in Schell's death. After learning how Schell died, Nash decides this is the way Ivy will die, by shotgun. When Ivy comes to town Nash is waiting, and in the showdown in the street Nash brings up his shotgun in time to beat Ivy's drawing of his revolver. Afterwards Connie tells Nash how sorry she is but he is unmoved. Instead he goes to Rose.

Ramrod verges on being a *film noir* western. Russell Harlan's stark black-and-white photography of the Arizona settings adds to the drama and the menacing quality of much of the action. The playing of veterans Preston Foster, Donald Crisp and Wesley Ruggles is another asset, and the performance of McCrea as the honest cowboy who has had his share of trouble is touching. It is clearly the work of a man who knows his way around a ranch. McCrea's reservations about the film stemmed from the casting of Veronica Lake, who was then married to director de Toth, "When you work with the director's wife, it's for the birds." He feels the part of the manipulative, slightly evil Connie needed a more subtle actress, someone of the quality of a Barbara Stanwyck.

FOUR FACES WEST

United Artists, 1948;
Produced by Harry Sherman; Directed by Alfred E. Green; Written by Graham Baker and Teddi Sherman, adapted by William and Milarde Brent from the novel *Paso por Aqui* by Eugene Manlove Rhodes; Photographed by Russell Harlan; Music by Paul Sawtell; 90 minutes.

Cast:
Ross McEwen, Joel McCrea; *Fay Hollister*, Frances Dee; *Pat Garrett*, Charles Bickford; *Monte Marquis*, Joseph Calleia; *Sheriff Egan*, William Conrad; *Florencia*, William Garralaga; *Doctor Elridge*, Raymond Largey; *Prenger*, John Parrish; *Clint Waters*, Dan White; *Burnett*, Davison Clark; *Mrs. Winston*, Eva Novak; *Winston Boy*, George McDonald; *Anderson*, Houseley Stevenson; *Storekeeper*, Sam Flint; *Conductor*, Forrest Taylor.

With the success of *Ramrod*, Harry Sherman put into production a western he had long wanted to do, *Four Faces West*, based upon the story *Paso Por Acqi*, which Eugene Manlove Rhodes had written for the Saturday Evening Post. Rhodes had been a cowboy before becoming a successful writer and western buffs regard his tales of western life as being more authentic and sympathetic than the average. This was clearly so in the case of *Paso Por Acqi*, which was so distinctly different that Sherman would probably not have gone ahead had it not been for the positive public reaction to the slightly offbeat *Ramrod*. Now it seemed there was a market for a more sensible kind of western. The film went into production under the translated title *They Passed This Way*, which was retained for the British release. For the role of the gentle robber whose story this is, Sherman had only Joel McCrea in

With Charles Bickford.

With Francis Dee.

mind. In fact, *Four Faces West* is considered by many to be *the* Joel McCrea western.

The story begins as Ross McEwen (McCrea) rides into the little town of Roswell, New Mexico and proceeds to the bank, where only the banker is present. His staff and almost everyone else is attending a welcoming for the famed lawman Pat Garrett (Charles Bickford), now taking his new position as the sheriff. McEwen quietly pulls a gun and asks the banker to hand over a large amount of money, for which he leaves an IOU. The robbery is an act of desperation because McEwen needs the money to save his father's ranch.

McEwen rides away and later boards a train where he meets a nurse, Fay Hollister (Frances

With Dee and Joseph Calleia.

Dee), recently arrived from the East to join a hospital, and Monte Marquez (Joseph Calleia), a saloon owner and by nature a compassionate man. Both sense there is a special quality about McEwen. When Marquez hears about the robbery he assumes McEwen is the man, while at the same time he is puzzled as to how such a man could be a thief. Fay, who is falling in love with McEwen, realizes he is in trouble, but he refuses to talk about it. It is something he has to work out by himself.

Garrett and his posse pursue McEwen, who makes his way across the desert. He stops by a farm to exchange his exhausted horse for another and finds a Mexican family stricken with diphtheria. The father, himself in a state of collapse, begs for help for his wife and children. McEwen stays and nurses the family, until he becomes exhausted. It is in this condition that Garrett finds him, but while arresting him understands what McEwen has done. Garrett sends for medical aid and Fay later arrives. She too is impressed with this kindly robber, who by this time has already started to send back some of the money taken from the bank. Before taking him off for trial, at which Garrett promises to ask for clemency, the sheriff allows McEwen to meet with Fay and Marquez. By a huge rock upon which travelers have marked the words "paso por acqi," Marquez tells Fay that McEwen's name should be added, that he was a gentlemen and "he passed this way." And that he will be back.

Four Faces West holds the distinction of being the only western so far made in which not a single shot is fired or a fist thrown. It also marks the best teaming of McCrea with his wife, Frances Dee, and the rapport is obvious.

Sadly, this fine film became the last for Harry Sherman, who afterwards retired. He died in 1952 at the age of sixty-seven. Few film producers did more for the western than Sherman. His name might also be chisled on that rock near Gallop, New Mexico, where most of *Four Faces West* was filmed. The rock in the film is the real one, photographed by Russell Harlan, the man Sherman used for most of his westerns, including the best of the Hopalong Cassidy series.

The genuine regard for the West on the part of men like Eugene Manlove Rhodes, Harry Sherman, Russell Harlan and Joel McCrea is obvious in a film like *Four Faces West*. About McCrea, Sherman said, "Joel is the greatest natural western actor since Mix and Hart, and he's the first natural horseman I've ever seen. No trick rider, just a guy who knows how to sit on a horse with grace and authority."

SOUTH OF ST. LOUIS

Warner Bros, 1949;
Produced by Milton Sperling; Directed by Ray Enright;
Written by Zachary Gold and James R. Webb;
Photographed in Technicolor by Karl Freund; Music by
Max Steiner; 88 minutes.

Cast:
Kip Davis, Joel McCrea; *Rouge de Lisle*, Alexis Smith;
Charles Burns, Zachary Scott; *Deborah Miller*, Dorothy
Malone; *Lee Price*, Douglas Kennedy; *Jake Evarts*, Alan
Hale; *Luke Cottrell*, Victor Jory; *Slim Hansen*, Bob Steele;
Bronco, Art Smith; *Captain Jeffers*, Monte Blue; *Manuel*,
Nacho Galindo.

Ramrod and *Four Faces West* increased Joel Mc-
Crea's marketability, especially since he had now
made known his intention to specialize in westerns.
Warner Bros offered him the lead in a Technicolor
film, of the kind they had virtually patented with
Dodge City (1939), *San Antonio* (1945), *Cheyenne*
(1947) and *Silver River* (1948), all of which had sym-
phonically lively scores by Max Steiner. Since almost all of the film takes place in Texas during the

With Alexis Smith and Dorothy Malone.

Civil War, audiences might have pondered the title
South of St. Louis. Oddly the film makes no reference
to "south of St. Louis" as being a term used in both
the Union and Confederate armies for desertion, a
term which later evolved into "going over the hill."
However, it is unlikely that the audiences for this
kind of western spent much time discussing the
title. This is not a "thinking man's" western.

In Missouri in the latter part of the Civil War,
Luke Cottrell (Victor Jory) leads a guerilla band for
the Union Army but pillages for his own profit.
Among those who suffer a loss are the three owners
of a burned-out ranch, Kip Davis (McCrea), Charlie
Burns (Zachary Scott) and Lee Price (Douglas Kennedy). They take off for Texas where Kip's bride-to-
be, Deborah (Dorothy Malone), is already headed.
They all settle in the border town of Brownsville,
where a saloon singer, Rouge de Lisle (Alexis
Smith), is a Confederate sympathizer involved in
smuggling guns. She employs Davis to work for
her, and later, Burns also agrees to work for her,
although his interest is purely financial. Price decides to join the Confederate Army.

As the war goes on Davis becomes more and
more involved in contraband and less ethical in his
associations, causing Deborah to lose faith in him
and to find a love more to her liking with the
upright Price. By the end of the war Burns has
decided that the life of an opportunistic businessman is what he wants, not a return to ranching, so
he leaves Davis. When Price returns he joins the
Texas Rangers, putting him at odds with Burns and
the group he represents—with Davis drifting somewhere between. Cottrell now operates in Texas but
Davis catches up with him and settles the old score.
Afterward, he crosses the river into Mexico and
drinks away his time in the company of Rouge, who
loves him but cannot straighten him out. His re-
demption comes when Deborah begs him to return
to Texas to stop a group led by Burns from killing
Price. In the final showdown Burns has a change of
heart and leaps to the side of his two old friends,
but loses his life in the process. With that Davis
resolves to make a life for himself with Rouge.

South of St. Louis is simply a slam-bang Civil War
western, slickly put together by Warner Bros with
the skill evident in all their westerns of this kind.
McCrea is a conventional hero in a part calling for
little interpretation. Of some interest to Civil War
buffs are the allusions the film makes to the British
and French business interests in supporting the Con-
federates. However, those considerations quickly
sink below the surface of a film swamped with

With Douglas Kennedy.

106

fighting and wild characters. A much more interesting Warner western was in the offing for McCrea.

COLORADO TERRITORY

Warner Bros, 1949;
Produced by Anthony Veiller; Directed by Raoul Walsh; Written by John Twist and Edmund H. North, based on the novel *High Sierra* by W. R. Burnett; Photographed by Sid Hickox; Music by David Buttolph; 94 minutes.

Cast:
Wes McQueen, Joel McCrea; *Colorado Carson*, Virginia Mayo; *Julie Ann*, Dorothy Malone; *Winslow*, Henry Hull; *Reno Blake*, John Archer; *Duke Harris*, James Mitchell; *Marshall*, Morris Ankrum; *Dave Rickard*, Basil Ruysdael; *Brother Tomas*, Frank Puglia; *Wallace*, Ian Wolfe; *Pluthner*, Harry Woods; *Prospector*, Houseley Stevenson; *Sheriff*, Victor Killian; *Station Agent*, Oliver Blake.

Eight years after directing Humphrey Bogart in *High Sierra* (1941), Warners asked Raoul Walsh to make the story again, this time as a western with John Wayne. Since Wayne was already committed to another project, Walsh suggested Joel McCrea, whom Warners approved immediately. Knowing that the actor had often been the second choice on other projects, Walsh asked McCrea if it bothered him on this particular project. McCrea shook his head. "No. When the picture opens, I'll be the guy that's riding out there - people won't know how many were up for the part." With that McCrea started work on what would become one of the finest of his westerns.

Instead of gangster Roy Earle as in *High Sierra*, the protagonist in *Colorado Territory* is outlaw Wes McQueen. While serving twenty years for bank and train robberies, he breaks out of jail and heads for Colorado to join his old gang, headed by crippled Dave Rickard (Basil Ruysdael). He eludes the hounding lawmen and en route comes across a stagecoach. The coach is attacked, the driver and guard killed, but McQueen saves the lives of the passengers, a man named Winslow (Henry Hull) and his daughter Julie Ann (Dorothy Malone). When McQueen arrives at the gang's hide-out, he finds there are two new members - Reno Blake (John Archer) and Duke Harris (James Mitchell). McQueen takes an instinctive disliking to both.

With Virginia Mayo.

With Dorothy Malone.

With Virginia Mayo.

With James Mitchell and John Archer.

With them is a half-breed girl, Colorado Carson (Virginia Mayo) with whom he feels mutual rapport.

McQueen tells Rickard that he has no futher interest in the gang, but the old man, himself wanting to end his career as a criminal, talks him into doing one last job, one that might bring the gang $100,000. McQueen successfully pulls off the job, despite the efforts of Blake and Harris to doublecross the gang and leave McQueen in the lurch. But McQueen outwits them and kills them both. Finding that old Rickard has died, he decides to find a new life for himself with Colorado. They stop off at the Winslow house, where Julie Ann tries to betray McQueen for the posted reward money, but Colorado senses the trap. She amd McQueen extricate themselves and take off for the Mexican border with a posse in pursuit. The geography is against them and they find themselves locked in a vast canyon. They take refuge in an old Indian dwelling but there is no escape. McQueen is wounded and when Colorado runs out to try to surrender on his behalf she is shot down. She and McQueen die together.

Colorado Territory is a classy western, thanks to the tough direction of the veteran Walsh, reputedly one of the more macho of directors, and the quiet, controlled performance by McCrea as the outlaw with a certain sense of dignity and his own code of honor. The stark black-and-white photography of Sid Hickox is a major asset, especially in the closing sequences in which the immensity of the setting dwarfs the humans, contrasting their insignificance against nature. The film has drive and emotional impact rare in most westerns. Walsh filmed in New Mexico, where he was able to use a genuine, old-fashioned narrow-gauged railroad for the robbery sequence, and actual Indian dwellings for the ending.

McCrea's portrayal of the doomed outlaw brought him more praise than usual, and for which he credited Walsh. "I'd do stuff for him that I wouldn't have done for any other director. He was a gutty little bastard. And funny. In the opening scene where I was escaping from prison, I had to run through a swamp with dogs after me. There were logs and rocks in it, and I fell down several times and damn near broke my leg, but I kept going because he was yelling 'keep running, kid, keep running.' When I came out the other end, muddy, wet, cold and out of breath. I looked for Walsh, expecting him to tell me how great I'd been and if it had been any other actor he would have used a double. But he wasn't there. The assistant director said Walsh left halfway through the run, telling him it looked good and use it. That's the way he'd do things. What a character!"

109

THE OUTRIDERS

MGM, 1950;
Produced by Richard Goldstone; Directed by Roy
Rowland; Written by Irving Ravetch; Photographed in
Technicolor by Charles Schoenbaum; Music by Andre
Previn; 93 minutes.

Cast:
Will Owen, Joel McCrea; *Jan Gort*, Arlene Dahl; *Jesse
Wallace*, Barry Sullivan; *Roy Gort*, Claude Jarmin, Jr.;
Clint Priest, James Whitmore; *Don Antonio Chaves*,
Ramon Novarro; *Keeley*, Jeff Corey; *Bye*, Ted De Corsia;
Father Damasco, Martin Garralaga;

With *The Outriders*, it was back to the Civil War
for Joel McCrea, in a handsome MGM Production
which included much location shooting in the re-
gion of Kanab, Utah, with its starkly beautiful vistas
of reddish, purplish canyons and mesas. Whereas
McCrea's adventures as Kip Davis in *South of St.
Louis* had been a little confusing in an overly complex plot, those of Will Owen, a captured Confederate sergeant, are relatively straight forward.

At Fort Benton, Missouri, in the last year of the
war, Owen, Jesse Wallace (Barry Sullivan) and Clint
Priest (James Whitmore) escape when a contingent
of Confederate prisoners is taken to a nearby lake to
bathe. They elude the Union Army pursuers and
steal horses from a farm, but they are soon captured
by a group of southern guerillas led by Keeley (Jeff
Corey), an officer in Quantrell's Brigade. Keeley
offers them the choice of being shot or joining his
band of marauders. Having heard about their mur-
derous rampages, Owen is not happy about the
choice but realizes he has to make it. He, Wallace
and Priest are instructed to head for Santa Fe, New
Mexico, where Don Antonio Chavez (Ramon Novarro) is due to leave with a wagon train containing
a million dollars worth of gold intended for the
Federal Treasury in St. Louis.

The three men follow the wagon train and save it
when it is attacked by Indians. They then offer their
services as protective outriders, although their intention is to lead it into a prearranged ambush with
Keeley and his group. Tension is caused by the
presence in the train of a beautiful widow, Jan Gort
(Arleen Dahl), to whom both Owen and Wallace are
drawn. The tension escalates when Jan's young
nephew Roy (Claude Jarman, Jr.) panics when giv-
en night sentry duty and causes the horses to stampede into the camp. A few days later Roy dies when
swept away during a river crossing. All the while

With James Whitmore and Barry Sullivan.

With Arlene Dahl.

With director Roy Rowland and Dahl.

the feeling between Owen and Wallace grows more bitter, with Wallace making his play for Jan obvious and Owen restraining himself.

When they learn from a farmer that the war is over, Wallace insists that they keep the rendezvous with Keeley, with whom he is in league. Owen realizes they have no intention of turning the gold over to the Confederacy, so he takes Wallace prisoner and ties him up, but Wallace persuades one of the others to let him go. With that he joins Keeley in ambushing the wagon train. In the ensuing skirmish Owen uses military tactics to defeat Keeley and his men. Afterward, he tracks Wallace into the woods where Wallace pretends to be out of ammunition, but Owen guesses he is not, and moves in for the kill.

While being far from a great Civil War western, *The Outriders* is a solidly good one, crafted with MGM care, including an interesting music score by Andre Previn. The best scenes are those between McCrea and the ever dependable Barry Sullivan, playing a cynical, selfish man. When he tells the McCrea character that their long, supposed friendship is over he is told, "Jesse, I'm gonna flood the prairie and wash away the gulleys with my tears." It is the kind of line McCrea could utter with a pokerfaced ease verging on gospel.

STARS IN MY CROWN

MGM, 1950;
Produced by William H. Wright; Directed by Jacques Tourneur; Written by Margaret Fitts, from an adaptation by Joe David Brown of his novel; Photographed by Charles Schienbaum; Music by Adolph Deutsch; 89 minutes.

Cast:
Josiah Doziah Gray, Joel McCrea; *Harriett Gray*, Ellen Drew; *John Kenyon*, Dean Stockwell; *Jeb Isbell*, Alan Hale; *Dr. D. K. Harris, Sr.*, Lewis Stone; *Dr. D. K. Harris, Jr.*, James Mitchell; *Faith Radmore Samuels*, Amanda Blake; *Uncle Famous Prill*, Juano Hernandez; *Sam Houston Jones*, Charles Kemper; *Sarah Isbell*, Connie Gilchrist; *Lon Backett*, Ed Begley; *Perry Lokey*, Jack Lambert; *Chloroform Wiggans*, Arthur Hunnicutt;

Although it is usually listed as a western, *Stars in My Crown* has nothing to do with the West. Instead it is set in a small southern town and tells of a parson who is good with his fists, yet knows how to use a gun when necessary. He solves a lot of hard problems, including facing up to the Ku Klux Klan. It was an excellent vehicle for Joel McCrea and finely directed by the French-born Jacques Tourneur, who had already made a name for himself directing a pair of classy horror movies, *Cat People* and *I Walked with a Zombie* (both in 1943) as well as the acclaimed *film noir Out of the Past* (1947).

Stars in My Crown is episodic in structure, being more a series of vinettes than a story. The title is drawn from the hymn of the same name, which is used throughout the film to back up the folksey, "come to the meeting" spirit instilled in the community by Josiah Doziah Gray (McCrea). It starts with his arrival with his wife Harriett (Ellen Drew) and son John (Dean Stockwell) shortly after the Civil War. Gray is a hearty, cheerful man, as ready with a quote from his bible as with his fists whenever physical persuasion is more in order. The townspeople have never come across a parson like this before and he soon wins most of them over to his side.

Gray finds much of his time spent in trying to break down prejudices, among them the town's resistance to the new attitudes of young doctor D. K. Harris (James Mitchell). They prefer the ways of

With Alan Hale and Dean Stockwell.

With Dean Stockwell and Ellen Drew.

his father (Lewis Stone), with whom they have grown up. Gray comes to the rescue of an elderly black man (Juano Hernandez) when the man is being ousted from the small plot of land on which he had always lived. Gray promotes courtships in the community, partly by offering the happy relationships he has with his wife as an example. When a traveling carnival comes to town, Gray encourages the enjoyment. When typhoid breaks out and panics the community, it is the tough pastor who calms the situation, and helps the young doctor establish his worth. But the thing that really brings Gray respect is the way he shames a masked mob of Ku Klux Klanners into backing down from an attempted lynching.

Stars in My Crown is one of the stars in the crown of Joel McCrea. The role of the strong, likeable pastor fits him like a glove. It is quintessential McCrea, thoroughly American and straight as an arrow. This pastor is no mere Holy Joe; when he strides into a saloon and slams a pistol on the bar the patrons pay attention. And when he faces down the Klanners there is no doubt that this is the man who could do it. He knows about prejudice and greed and ignorance, and how to do something about it. Josiah Doziah Gray is Joel McCrea at his best.

112

TALES OF THE TEXAS RANGERS

NBC, 1950—1952

Like all movie stars in the pre-television era, Joel McCrea "appeared" on radio, mostly in sound versions of movies devised for the greatly popular *Lux Radio Theatre* produced and hosted by Cecil B. DeMille. The only series in which McCrea starred was *Tales of the Texas Rangers*, which was aired for the first time on July 8, 1950. The program ran as a weekly half-hour over the next two years. McCrea voiced the role of Ranger Jace Pearson in stories that were claimed to be based on actual case histories. The producers stated that for obvious reasons, names and dates had to be changed, but they maintained the stories were true. The modestly successful radio series was mostly written by Joel Murcott, and produced and directed by Stacey Keach.

SADDLE TRAMP

Universal, 1950;
Produced by Leonard Goldstein; Directed by Hugo Fregonese; Written by Harold Shumate; Photographed in Technicolor by Charles P. Boyle; Music direction: Joseph Gershenson; 77 minutes.

Cast:
Chuck Connor, Joel McCrea; *Della,* Wanda Hendrix; *Rocky,* John Russell; *Jess Higgins,* John McIntire; *Ma Higgins,* Jeanette Nolan; *Pop,* Russell Simpson; *Mr. Hartnagle,* Ed Begley; *Robbie,* Jimmy Hunt; *Tommy,* Orley Lindgren; *Johnnie,* Gordon Gebert; *Butch,* Gregory Moffett; *Martinez,* Antonio Moreno; *Slim,* John Ridgely;

Any western that includes in its opening sequence the question, "Which way'd they go?" and the reply, "Thataway!" must either be a tired, old cliche or one with an attitude of sly humor on the part of the makers. *Saddle Tramp* is happily one of the latter kind, and one in which Joel McCrea is fully at ease as an ambling cowboy - until fate forces him into the role of foster father. The screenplay, an original by the veteran scripter of western tales

Harold Shumate, and the straight-on direction of the Argentina-born, former journalist Hugo Fregonese make this a beguiling western. It was Fregonese's second American film, following the excellent *One Way Street* (1950).

Carefree drifter Chuck Connor (McCrea) is a man content to leave responsibility to others. While visiting a friend and his four motherless boys, the father is accidentally killed. Since they have no one else to turn to, Connor takes the four under his wing, which forces him to look for work. He finds a job on the ranch of Jess Higgins (John McIntire), a crusty man who dislikes children. Connor hides his group in the nearby woods, feeding them with food he steals from Mrs. Higgins kitchen. His worries increase with the arrival of nineteen-year-old Della (Wanda Hendrix) who has run away from the home of her guardian, a lecherous uncle (Ed Begley). The boys decide she should become one of the group, with Connor having to agree. It also means having to steal just a little more food until the kindly Mrs. Higgins (Jeanette Nolan) finds the reason for the theft and aleviates the need.

The feeding of the children is a minor problem compared to the rustling that has been bothering Higgins. He believes that his neighbor, Martinez

With Wanda Hendrix.

(Antonio Moreno) is the culprit, but Martinez is also losing cattle and suspects Higgins. Connor pokes around and discovers that the real culprits are the foremen of the two ranches, working together to steal from their respective bosses. Connor catches up with the Higgins' foreman (John Russell) and gives him a thrashing. With peace declared on the range Connor now has to figure out what to do about his own life. He soon realizes he is no longer a free-wheeling individual. Della suggests that they get married and head for California, with the four boys sent to school under the supervision of Mr. and Mrs. Higgins, he no longer quite so anti-children.

The leisurely paced *Saddle Tramp*, spiked here and there with some wild riding, cattle stampeding and brawling, is yet another western in which Joel McCrea does not fire a gun, or even draw it from its holster. Indeed, his Chuck Connor is about as amiable a cowpoke as there ever was, making his marriage to a young girl a little suspect. The musical score includes a song popular in 1950, "The Call of a Wild Goose," which serves as a kind of spiritual motif for the hero. At the end, as he and his child bride ride away, and the music swells up, a gaggle of wild geese fly overhead. He looks up wistfully. Is this a man likely to settle down?

FRENCHIE

Universal, 1950;
Produced by Michel Kraike; Directed by Louis King; Written by Oscar Brodney; Photographed in Technicolor; Music by Hans Salter; 81 minutes.

Cast:
Tom Banning, Joel McCrea; *Frenchie Fontaine*, Shelley Winters; *Pete Lambert*, Paul Kelly; *Countess*, Elsa Lanchester; *Diane*, Marie Windsor; *Lance Cole*, John Russell; *Clyde Gorman*, John Emery; *Jeff Harding*, George Cleveland; *Carter*, Regis Toomey; *Rednose*, Paul E. Burns; *Jim Dobbs*, Frank Ferguson; *Tony*, Vincent Renno; *Bartender*, Larry Dobkin; *Dealer*, Lucille Barkley;

The credit titles of Universal's *Frenchie* make no allusions to the story by Max Brand, *Destry Rides Again*, which they had first filmed with Tom Mix in 1932, and which they remade in 1939 with James Stewart and Marlene Dietrich. They would trot it out again five years after *Frenchie* as *Destry*, with Audie Murphy. The similarities are many, including a sheriff, this time Joel McCrea, who softens the flinty heart of a lady saloon keeper, this time Shelley Winters, in a rough little town called Bottleneck (same as in the 1939 *Destry Rides Again*), and an extended brawl between the lady and a wife of one

With Shelley Winters.

An accident on location near Bishop, California, while filming **Frenchie.** *Winters was badly bruised and shaken, but otherwise not hurt. The rig in which they were riding overturned after hitting a soft shoulder.*

of the saloon's clients, in this conflict Marie Windsor. For all that the only scenarist credited with *Frenchie* is Oscar Brodney.

The Brodney screenplay changes the shy, pacifist sheriff of the 1939 version into the stong but mild mannered Tom Banning (McCrea), a sheriff who goes by the letter of the law. And unlike Dietrich's rootless saloon hostess Frenchy, Shelley Winter's Frenchie Fontaine is a lady with a purpose. She has returned to Bottleneck fifteen years after the murder of her father with revenge in mind. Now a successful New Orleans gambling house operator, she has enough money to buy a casino in Bottleneck. She soon meets Banning, who although he knows why she has returned, can not help becoming fond of her, or vice versa. Frenchie is certain that one of the two men who killed her father is saloon operator Pete Lambert (Paul Kelly), but she does not know the identity of his partner in crime.

Suspicion as to the identity begin to dawn on Frenchie when she comes into conflict with Diane (Windsor), the wife of banker Clyde Gorman (John

Emery). Diane is in love with Banning and when she suspects that Banning is falling for Frenchie, she becomes indiscreet, especially after a vicious brawl with Frenchie. The clues point to Gorman as the other man, which leads to his being murdered. Banning is accused of the murder and arrested, but Frenchie, convinced of his innocence, helps him escape. He, on the other hand, is sure that Frenchie is the killer of Gorman. Lambert stages a gunfight hoping to get rid of Frenchie and Banning, but it is one in which both he and Diane are mortally wounded. Before she dies Diane admits she killed her husband, leaving Frenchie and Banning free to be together in peace.

Frenchie is a slickly made but unremarkable western, with no great effort required by either star. By 1950, Shelley Winters was already an expert in playing hard shelled but soft hearted ladies, and for McCrea to play a strong, quiet peace officer was no harder for him than getting on and off a horse, as anyone offering him this kind of picture well knew.

HOLLYWOOD STORY

Universal, 1951;
Produced by Leonard Goldstein; Directed by William Castle; Written by Frederick Kohner and Fred Brady; Photographed by Carl Guthrie; Music by Joseph Gershenson; 76 minutes.

Cast:
Larry O'Brien, Richard Conte; *Sally Rousseau,* Julia Adams; *Lt. Lennox,* Richard Egan; *Vincent St. Clair,* Henry Hull; *Sam Collyer,* Fred Clarke; *Mitch Davis,* Jim Backus; *Roland Paul,* Paul Cavanagh; *and guest stars:* Joel McCrea, Francis X. Bushman, William Farnum, Betty Blythe and Helen Gibson

Between the release of *Frenchie* in November of 1950 and his next western for Universal, *Cattle Drive* (July, 1951), Joel McCrea was fleetingly seen in the studio's *Hollywood Story*. For those interested in the movies that Hollywood has made about Hollywood, this one is especially interesting. Its scenario is based on the notorious and unsolved murder of director William Desmond Taylor in 1922. It presents Richard Conte in the role of Larry O'Brien, a producer who becomes intrigued with the case and decides to make a movie about it. In the course of so doing, O'Brien visits many old Hollywood locations, hotels, and restaurants. He hires as his base of operation the old Chaplin Studio on La Brea Avenue.

At one point in the story, O'Brien visits the Universal Studios to interview an old actor named Roland Paul (Paul Cavanagh), a former silent star now making a living as a character player. The actor is about to play a scene as a doctor in a western starring McCrea. As he and O'Brien talk, McCrea emerges from his dressing room, asks O'Brien how he is progressing with his film and then plays a brief scene with Paul. The scene, barely half a minute in length, was written for *Hollywood Story* and is not part of any other McCrea film.

CATTLE DRIVE

Universal, 1951;
Produced by Aaron Rosenberg; Directed by Kurt Neumann; Written by Jack Nattleford and Lillie Hayward; Photographed in Technicolor by Maurie Gertsman; Music direction: Joseph Gershenson; 77 minutes.

Cast:
Dana Mathews, Joel McCrea; *Chester Graham, Jr.,* Dean Stockwell; *Dallas,* Chill Wills; *Mr. Graham,* Leon Ames; *Jim Currie,* Henry Brandon; *Cap,* Howard Petrie; *Careless,* Bob Steele; *Conductor O'Hara,* Griff Barnett;

Westerns that deviate from the norm are rare, and among those that do, it may be noted that quite a few feature Joel McCrea. When approached by a

With Dean Stockwell.

With Howard Petrie, Chill Wills, and Stockwell.

damage or loss and even the toughest of the cowboys take an understanding stance. By the end of the two weeks of trail driving, Chester has not only developed into a good worker but the edge has been taken off his arrogance and conceit. What the railroad tycoon gets back is a happily different son.

Cattle Drive, largely filmed amid spectacular locations in the vicinity of Death Valley and featuring some fine running shots of horses and cattle, is unusual in that it has no villains and no heroines. The only time a lady appears in the film is when McCrea pulls a wallet from his pocket and shows the boy a picture of the lady waiting at the end of the trail. In a nice touch, the picture happens to be one of Frances Dee (Mrs. McCrea). In the role of Dana Mathews, McCrea is fully at ease, with just the right touch of casualness for a natural-born cowboy, tough enough not to bend to the demands of a spoiled brat, but compassionate enough to want to set the boy straight. In fact, quite a bit like that fisherman in *Captains Courageous*.

producer the actor always wanted to know the story line and the kind of character he would be required to play. If the story was at all different, and if it showed westerners in a realistic light, then the producer had a good chance of getting McCrea to do it. *Cattle Drive* appealed to him, partly because it was about the business in which he was engaged when not acting. He might also have noticed that the plot bore some resemblance to *Captains Courageous* (1937), in which fishermen Spencer Tracy turns little snob Freddie Bartholomew into a better boy.

This is the tale of Chester Graham, Jr. (Dean Stockwell), the spoiled son of a railroad tycoon (Leon Ames), who misses his train after a watering stop in the Arizona desert and finds himself alone. Along comes Dana Mathews (McCrea) and his trail herd. The cocky young boy offers Mathews money if he will take him to his father, but Mathews explains his job is to get his herd to market. The best he can offer it to take the boy along, provided he is willing to work. At first offended, Chester gradually gets into the spirit of things and after a few days as a cowboy he finds he is enjoying it, although his opinions and values irk the rest of the group. The understanding Mathews comes to his resuce in a number of altercations.

Chester's worst moment comes when he sets loose a wild horse that frightens the cattle, causing a stampede. However, the stampede results in no real

THE SAN FRANCISCO STORY

Warner Bros, 1952;
Produced by Howard Welsch; Directed by Robert Parrish; Written by D. D. Beauchamp, based on the novel by Richard Summers; Photographed by John Seitz; Music by Emil Newman and Paul Dunlap; 80 minutes.

Cast:
Rick Nelson, Joel McCrea; *Adelaide McCall*, Yvonne De Carlo; *Andrew Cain*, Sidney Blackmer; *Shorty*, Richard Erdman; *Saide*, Florence Bates; *Jim Martin*, Onslow Stevens; *Lessing*, John Raven; *Alfey*, O. Z. Whitehead; *Winfield Holbert*, Ralph Dumke; *Thompson*, Robert Foulk; *Morton*, Lane Chandler; *Miner*, Trevor Bardette; *Slade*, John Doucette; *Meyers*, Peter Virgo; *Palmer*, Frank Hagney; *Buck*, Tor Johnson; *Scud*, Fred Graham;

The San Francisco Story falls far short of what its title implies. It is not the history of a great city but simply a concocted tale about crime and vigilantes in 1856. In this entry, Joel McCrea is Rick Nelson, a successful miner who comes to visit his newspaper publisher friend Jim Martin (Onslow Stevens), and finds the city as full of crime as when he left five years previously. He was then himself a vigilante but now he turns down Martin's plea to become one again. Nelson is in town to enjoy himself.

With Yvonne De Carlo.

Martin, head of the vigilante committee, is mostly concerned about powerful crook Andrew Cain (Sidney Blackmer). Cain lives elegantly and manages to control local politics by his manipulation of officials, even on the senatorial level. Cain's stylish way of life includes a beautiful mistress, Adelaide McCall (Yvonne De Carlo), to whom Nelson takes an immediate shine and begins to pay too much attention. She responds with enough interest to cause Cain to have Nelson shanghaied and dumped in the bowels of a ship in the harbor. Nelson manages to fight his way out and swim back the to wharfs. He goes to see Cain and surprises him with the idea that he would like to become a partner in Cain's operation. Even Adelaide is suspicious, to which Cain responds, "I said I'd use him, not believe him."

As a token of good faith Nelson agrees to break a Cain underling from jail. The man is shot down once outside and Nelson himself is hit by gunfire. Wounded and hauled into seclusion by his friend Shorty (Richard Erdman), Nelson asks Martin to publish a false account of his death. This gives Cain the confidence to proceed with his plan to fix a political campaign, but it also causes Adelaide, now in love with Nelson, to go to Martin with documentary evidence of Cain's crimes.

Once recovered from his wound Nelson faces Cain in public and challenges him, leaving Cain the choice of weapons. Cain chooses shotguns. On a wide sandy beach the next morning the two face each other on horseback. Cain's planted marksman misses Nelson and is shot by Shorty as Nelson blasts Cain out of his saddle. Afterward, Nelson and Adelaide leave for his home in the mining country.

The plotlines of *The San Francisco Story* are conventional, although it is possibly the only western in which the hero is shanghaied, and one of the few in which there are coastal sequences. The hero is also a somewhat better humored man than the usual McCrea western hero, and the dialogue a cut above average in wit. When the publisher friend suggests to McCrea that if he wants an enjoyable evening he might consider a social being given by a ladies' church group, he replies with ernestness, "I wanted to have a good time but, golly, I didn't want to go *that* far." And as Adelaide goes to kiss him after he has escaped the shanghai experience to which she was a party he demurs, "I don't think I'd better kiss you tonight, Addie - it hasn't been working out too well." These bits of bantering are handled by McCrea with a deft, dry, alomst Sturgian style.

ROUGH SHOOT

United Artists, 1953;
Produced by Raymond Stross; Directed by Robert Parrish; Written by Eric Ambler, based on a novel by Geoffrey Household; Photographed by Stanley Pavey; Music by Hans May; 87 minutes.

Cast:
Lt. Col. Taine, Joel McCrea; *Cecily,* Evelyn Keyes; *Sandorski,* Herbert Lom; *Hiart,* Marius Goring; *Randall,* Roland Culver; *Diss,* Karel Stepanek; *Lex,* David Hurst; *Magda,* Patricia Laffen; *Hassingham,* Frank Lawton; *Mrs. Powell,* Megs Jenkins; *Blossom,* Laurence Naismith; *Cartwright,* Cyril Raymond; *Inspector Sullivan,* Clement McCallin; *Inspector Matthews,* Jack McNaughton; *Sergean Bains,* Arnold Bell;

Joel McCrea made only one film outside of the United States, the espionage thriller *Rough Shoot,* made in England. Despite two stars and a director, Robert Parrish, brought from Hollywood it is essentially an English movie. It turned out to be a disappointment to both McCrea and the public, who had reason to expect more from a screenplay written by a master of this genre, Eric Ambler. The end result was a modestly intriguing piece of entertainment with McCrea as an American Army Lieutenant Colonel, stationed in England and living in the countryside of Dorset with his wife.

The murky picture opens during a dark night when Taine (McCrea) and his wife Cecily (Evelyn Keyes) are disturbed by the sound of a prowler. Taine takes a shotgun, goes outside and fires at the figure. He kills what he assumes is a poacher, then panics and hides the body, puzzled as to how he could have killed the man with a round of buckshot.

Taine is soon visited by Sandorski (Herbert Lom), a mysterious, flamboyant Pole, who claims military rank and tells Taine that he is involved with British Intelligence. He also says that he is a witness to the killing and that he will keep quiet if Taine will work with him in espionage. Sandorski's apparent assignment is to round up spies trying to locate atomic data. It turns out that the assumed poacher was one of those spies and that it was Sandorski who killed him, timing his shot with that of Taine's shotgun blast. Before that disclosure Taine is drawn into a dangerous and complicated pursuit of the spies, culminating in their capture in the Madame Taussauds Waxworks in London.

Rough Shoot did not impress reviewers on either side of the Atlantic. The consesus was that it was too muddled and improbable for its own good, a film for which it was hardly necessary to drag Joel McCrea all the way from Hollywood. The pity is that this one film made by McCrea outside of the United States could not have been better, and its mild reception probably convinced him that it would be better to go back to California and stick with westerns.

With Herbert Lom.

With Evelyn Keyes and Roland Culver.

THE LONE HAND

Universal, 1953;
Produced by Howard Christie; Directed by George
Sherman; Written by Joseph Hoffman, based on a story
by Irving Ravetch; Photographed in Technicolor by
Maury Gertsman; Music direction: Joseph Gershenson;
80 minutes.

Cast:
Zachary Halleck, Joel McCrea; *Sarah Jane Skaggs,* Barbara
Hale; *Jonah Varden,* Alex Nicol; *George Hadley,* Charles
Drake; *Joshua,* Jimmy Hunt; *Gus Varden,* Jim Arness; *Mr.
Skaggs,* Roy Roberts; *Mr. Dunn,* Frank Ferguson; *Daniel
Skaggs,* Wesley Morgan;

Back in California after having made a not very
successful non-western in England, Joel McCrea
signed with Universal to do three westerns, returning him to the genre from which he would never
again deviate. The first was *The Lone Hand,* directed
by the veteran George Sherman, who began his
career directing B westerns. The result was an
above average entry, with a good script based on an
Irving Ravetch story, although one employing the
long familiar device of the hero who poses as a
bandit in order to round up the gang.

Widower Zachary Halleck (McCrea) comes to
the town of Timberlane with his son Joshua (Jimmy
Hunt), to buy a small, rundown farm. They find
that the area is plagued with robberies and killings,
and that the local vigilante committee is unable to

With Jimmy Hunt.

cope with the situation. Halleck is asked to join the
committee but refuses, much to the surprise of his
son, who idolizes his father. He had described to his
father how he saw outlaws kill a detective of the
Pinkerton Agency. Halleck courts and weds Sarah
Jane (Barbara Hale) and goes about running his
farm, which includes buying a lot of equipment.

Both the source of Halleck's money and his un-
explained absences puzzle his wife and son, especially since robberies occur during those periods.
Joshua is amazed to witness his father taking part in
a robbery with the men who killed the detective.
The strange absences continue and eventually his
wife concludes that Halleck is one of the outlaws,
and leaves him, taking Joshua with her. The aliena-
tion with his family ends when Halleck brings the
outlaws to justice and reveals his true identity. He is
a Pinkerton detective, who has been acting under-
cover to smoke out the leader of the local crime
wave, who turns out to be the affable and hitherto
respected horse rancher George Hadley (Charles
Drake).

The Lone Hand was in the hands of one of Universal's top producers, Howard Christie, who took his
cast and crew to the area in and around Durango,
Colorado, where the beautiful *mise-en-scene* was
deftly color photographed by Maury Gertsman.
And like all McCrea westerns, the emphasis was
upon authenticity of style, costume and manner
rather than merely on action.

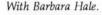

With Barbara Hale.

BORDER RIVER

Universal, 1954;
Produced by Albert J. Cohen; Directed by George
Sherman; Written by Louis Stevens and William
Sackheim; Photographed in Technicolor by Irving
Glassberg; Music direction: Joseph Gershenson; 81
minutes.

Cast:
Clete Mattson, Joel McCrea; *Carmelita Carias*, Yvonne De
Carlo; *General Callejo*, Pedro Armendariz; *Newland*,
Howard Petrie; *Annina Strasser*, Erika Nordin; *Captain
Vargas*, Alfonso Bedoya; *Sanchez*, George J. Lewis; *Lopez*,
Nacho Galindo; *Baron von Hollden*, Ivan Triesault;
Fletcher, George Wallace; *Stanton*, Joe Bassett; *Guzman*,
Martin Garralaga; *Anderson*............. Lane Chandler
Pablo, Felipe Turich; *Crowe*, Charles Horvath; *General
Robles*, Salvador Baguez;

George Sherman was also the director of *Border
River*, Joel McCrea's next Universal adventure,
which took the actor back to the Civil War. His co-
star is Yvonne De Carlo, bringing them together
again two years after their pairing in *The San Francisco Story*. Just as she was the mistress of the villain
in that film so she is again a mistress in this one.
What makes *Border River* of more than usual interest
is that the action takes place in an area of Mexico
that broke off from that country and became for

some years an independent territory, the Zona Libre
on the other side of the Rio Grande. It was the result
of the war between the forces of Benito Juarez and
those of Maximilian, the Austrian Emperor in-
stalled by the French, and in those years which
coincided with the American Civil War, it was a
refuge for American deserters and for businessmen
supplying arms in every direction.

Border River begins in Colorado, as Confederate
Major Clete Mattson (McCrea) and his men steal
two million dollars worth of gold bullion from a
Federal mint. The money is desperately needed by
the South in this final year of the war. With it
Mattson proceeds to Zona Libre to make deals for
arms and ammunition. News of the robbery cause
conflicts with a number of parties trying to acquire
it, both en route and in the zone. His main oppo-
nent becomes the renegade Mexican general Callejo
(Pedro Armendariz), the most powerful man in the
zone and one who has grown rich on the taxes he
levies on crooks hiding out under his protection.

Callejo does all he can to wrest the gold from
Mattson. The conflict is made the more bitter after
Mattson meets Callejo's glamorous girlfriend Carmelita (De Carlo), who operates a saloon. Through
the love that grows between Mattson and Carmelita, she begins to lose the cynicism brought
about by the death of her father and brother in

With Yvonne De Carlo.

With Pedro Armendariz and De Carlo.

next adventure Out West. They would do exactly that.

BLACK HORSE CANYON

Universal, 1954;
Produced by John W. Rogers; Directed by Jesse Hibbs;
Written by Geoffrey Holmes, based on a story by Lee Savage, Jr.
Photographed in Technicolor by George Robinson;
Music direction: Joseph Gershenson; 81 minutes.

Cast:
Del Rockwell, Joel McCrea; *Aldis Spain*, Mari Blanchard; *Ti*, Race Gentry; *Jennings*, Murvyn Vye; *Doc*, Irving Bacon; *Duke*, John Pickard; *Sheriff*, Ewing Mitchell; *Juanita*, Pilar Del Rey; *Graves*, William J. Williams;

political skirmishes. She supports Mattson as he tries to get aid for the Confederacy, a struggle that includes not only Callejo but his venal German military advisor (Ivan Triesault), who wants the gold for himself, and the Union agents trying to stop Mattson. After much intrigue and fighting the time comes when Mattson and Callejo face each other man to man - with the inevitable results. The two fight while trapped in quicksand, with a contingent of troops from the Juarez army arriving in time to rescue the hero.

Border River is not a western to invite much comment. For 1954, it was solid entertainment, concocted by experts in this genre, including Joel McCrea, who was fully confident that Universal would hand him another well written script for his

Dealing as it does with horse ranching, *Black Horse Canyon* is a film for which rancher Joel Mc-Crea might well have been hired as technical advisor had he not been its star. Based on the novel *The Wild Horse* by Lee Savage, Jr., the story lines were not far removed from the actor's own experiences over the previous twenty years and the character of cowboy Del Rockwell was not one for which he needed to do any research.

The film's protagonist is not a human but a horse, a black stallion that runs wild through the hills and is of such vibrant sex appeal that mares on

With Race Gentry and Mari Blanchard.

various ranches answer his call and follow him. This outlaw equine was once the property of strong-willed young stock rancher, Aldis Spain (Mari Blanchard), who runs a ranch with her uncle Doc (Irving Bacon). She wants the stallion back, and other ranchers, particularly one named Jennings (Murvyn Vye) would like to corral it for their own purposes. Among the others is Del Rockwell and his young English partner Ti (Race Gentry), who are trying to start up their own horse ranch. Aldis is able to persuade Rockwell to come in with her, to the chagrin of Jennings.

Rockwell is an easy-going, laconic, worldly-wise old cowboy, with a history as a ladies' man, as well as a bronc buster. The idea of getting both the stallion and the girl appeals to him, his main problem being Ti's own hankering for Aldis. As the three of them set out to round up the stallion, the two men cooperate concerning the horse but not the girl. Their efforts are complicated by the unscrupulous efforts of Jennings to grab the horse for himself, any way he can. When his efforts to hire Rockwell fail, Jennings has his men raid Rockwell's camp, which also fails. This failure leads him to have his men act as raiders. He also involves the sheriff with the charge that the horse is dangerous and therefore, should be shot. Nothing Jennings does gets him the horse, which Rockwell captures and breaks for the girl who has now decided she would like the cowboy as well as the stallion.

Black Horse Canyon is a horse lover's picture, with a gorgeous stallion that literally woos mares, but when angry, becomes a plunging mustang attacking those trying to capture him. In short, a horse that is both a lady killer and a man killer, and a joy to watch as he gallops around the Technicolor West.

In signing his three-film deal with Universal, McCrea had asked that each be as different as possible from the other. They had obliged. *The Lone Hand* was a western crime story, *Border River* had been historical in its setting, and *Black Horse Canyon* was a genuine cowboy picture. There is little doubt that the third saddle was the most comfortable one for McCrea.

STRANGER ON HORSEBACK

United Artists, 1955;
Produced by Robert Goldstein; Directed by Jacques Tourneur; Written by Herb Meadow and Don Martin, based on the story by Louis L'Amour; Photographed in Ansco Color by Ray Rennahan; Music by Paul Dunlap; 66 minutes.

Cast:
Rick Thorne, Joel McCrea; *Amy Lee Bannerman*,Miroslava; *Tom Bannerman*, Kevin McCarthy; *Josiah Bannerman*, John McIntire; *Caroline Webb*, Nancy Gates; *Colonel Streeter*, John Carridine; *Sheriff Nat Bell*, Emile Meyer; *Arnold Hammer*, Robert Cornthwaite; *Vince Webb*, Walter Baldwin; *Paula Morison*, Jaclynne Greene;

After working with him on *Stars in My Crown*, Joel McCrea told director Jacques Tourneur he

125

With Miroslava.

would when the occasion presented itself, like to do another film with him. The chance came when producer Robert Goldstein gave McCrea his choice of director for *Stranger on Horseback*, with a screenplay based on the story by Louis L'Amour. The result was a taut western drama, albeit by 1955 standards an unusually short one. At 66 minutes it was the length of the average B western of years gone by. Tourneur opted for tight editing, a boon for viewers, in a story that presents McCrea as Circuit Judge Rick Thorne, a man of serious demeanor, for whom justice is an absolute doctrine.

In the course of making his rounds, Thorne comes to the town of Bannerman, which is dominated by an old-line family headed by Josiah Bannerman (John McIntire). The area is something akin to a feudal fiefdom and it has been without the services of a court judge for some time. When Thorne becomes curious about a mysterious death, he turns up evidence that implicates Bannerman's spoiled son Tom (Kevin McCarthy), and implies that Tom may also be responsible for other deaths, although never held to account. Tom claims the most recent incident was self defense, but that does not stop Thorne from arresting him, even with the threat of trouble from Josiah Bannerman.

Thorne's main problem is in finding witnesses in the town who have the courage to speak the truth. The doggedness with which Thorne goes about his task amazes the cowed sheriff, Nat Ball (Emile Meyer), who by siding with the judge starts to regain his self respect. The stand also wins him a certain degree of respect from Bannerman himself, who nevertheless brings all his weight to bear to save his son. Another ally proves to be Bannerman's daughter Amy Lee (Miroslava), who realizes her brother is guilty and who helps the judge get Tom to another town in order to get a fair trial. It is there that justice is done.

Photographed for the most part on location in Mexico by the veteran Ray Rennahan - some of his other credits include no less than *Gone With the Wind* (1939), *For Whom the Bell Tolls* (1943) and *Duel in the Sun* (1947) - *Stranger on Horseback* is a superb minor western. Much of the credit is due Tourneur, with whom McCrea had a good rapport. He had helped the actor to be an upstanding and believable preacher in *Stars in My Crown*, and the credibility of McCrea's circuit riding judge was no doubt aided by the director.

At the outset of production producer Robert Goldstein admitted to McCrea that he had not raised enough of the modest budget to pay him the

With John Carradine and Emil Meyer.

agreed upon salary. McCrea liked the script enough to proceed on the understanding that he would receive a quarter of the film's profits. In time that income more than matched the salary. What McCrea most remembered about *Stranger on Horseback* is the compliment received from novelist Louis L'Amour. "He told me that my playing of his character was exactly what he had in mind when he wrote it. I was very proud to hear that."

WICHITA

Allied Artists, 1955;
Produced by Walter Mirisch; Directed by Jacques Tourneur; Written by Daniel B. Ullman; Photographed in Cinemascope and Technicolor by Harold Lipstein; Music by Hans Salter; 80 minutes.

Cast:
Wyatt Earp, Joel McCrea; *Laurie*, Vera Miles; *Gyp*, Lloyd Bridges; *Whiteside*, Wallace Ford; *Doc Black*, Edgar Buchanan; *Morgon*, Peter Graves; *Bat Masterson*, Keith Larson; *Mayor*, Carl Benton Reid; *Jim*, John Smith; *McCoy*, Walter Coy; *Wallace*, Walter Sande; *Ben Thompson*, Robert Wilke; *Hal*, Rayford Barnes; *Mrs. McCoy*, Mae Clarke;

In 1955, Joel McCrea was approached by producer Walter Mirisch with the idea of doing a series of westerns budgeted around the half million dollar mark which would be released by Allied Artists.

With Vera Miles.

McCrea agreed to a non-exclusive contract and proceeded with *Wichita*, in which he would play the famed lawman Wyatt Earp. Part of the attraction of the Mirisch offer was the opportunity to portray a number of historical figures. McCrea was impressed with the first script, an original screenplay by Daniel B. Ullman, which had something to say about western business ethics. McCrea was again able to bring in Jacques Tourneur as director.

Wyatt Earp, who died in Los Angeles in 1929 at the age of eighty, had been portrayed in many movies prior to this one. His adventures as a peace-loving but deadly lawman from Kansas to California, had been chronicled by Stuart Lake, whose book *Frontier Marshall* became a film of that title with George O'Brien as Earp in 1934, and again with Randolph Scott in 1939. Earp was also played by Richard Dix in *Tombstone, The Town Too Tough to Die* (1942), and by Henry Fonda in John Ford's classic *My Darling Clementine* (1946). He had appeared as a secondary figure in other westerns, and even after the McCrea version, Earp would surface again in the guise of Burt Lancaster in *Gunfight at the O. K. Corral* (1957), and James Stewart in *Cheyenne Autumn* (1964), plus a popular television series

starring Hugh O'Brien. It is to McCrea's credit that his performance has to take a back seat to none of the others. It was said among those who knew Earp in Hollywood, including Tom Mix, that he was "a fine old gentleman," which is exactly what people said about Joel McCrea in his later years.

The characterization of Earp in *Wichita* is a noble one, a man concerned with civil rights (including those of women), a consideration not found in many westerns. To attract cattlemen to its shipping center in 1870, Wichita declared itself a wide open town. The film focuses with some accuracy on the civic fear caused by drunken cowboys celebrating their end-of-trail relaxation, and the compromising self-debasement which made the townspeople endure it in the name of profit.

The film begins with Earp refusing to accept the offered position of town marshall, but he changes his mind when a child is killed by a band of cowboys madly riding up and down the main street. He bans the carrying of guns in the town, both for visitors and citizens, and under his tough control the fear of danger dies down. But so does business, causing a delegation of businessmen to accuse Earp of having "gone too far." Chief among them is Doc

128

Black (Edgar Buchanan), who enlists outlaws to get rid of Earp.

On Earp's side is newspaper publisher Whiteside (Wallace Ford), whose eager young assistant Bat Masterson (Keith Larsen) offers to help Earp any way he can. Earp cautions him not to be too ready to get involved in conflicts with gunmen. Another conflict for Earp is his love for Laurie (Vera Miles), the daughter of the mayor (Walter Coy) who is now as keen to get rid of Earp as he was to hire him. Laurie is caught in the middle in her loyalties. Eventually it is the death of Laurie's mother (Mae Clarke) that brings the situation to a head. Earp defeats every attempt on his life, including the final one in which a band of cowboys instigated by Doc Black attack Earp while he is visiting Laurie. In the malee the mother is killed by a stray bullet. Earp's points about violence become obvious; the mayor changes his stand and the cattlemen retreat.

Wichita was well reviewed, with favorable comment on McCrea's dignified and stalwart interpretation of Wyatt Earp. The actor's new association with Walter Mirisch augered well.

With Wallace Ford and Keith Larsen.

With Walter Sande, Robert Wilke, Rayford Barnes, and Lloyd Bridges.

THE FIRST TEXAN

Allied Artists, 1956;
Produced by Walter Mirisch; Directed by Byron
Haskins; Written by Daniel B. Ullman; Photographed in
Cinemascope and Technicolor by Wilfred Cline; Music
by Roy Webb; 82 minutes.

Cast:
Sam Houston, Joel McCrea; *Katherine*, Felicia Farr; *Jim
Bowie*, Jeff Morrow; *Delaney*, Wallace Ford; *Don Carlos*,
Abraham Sofaer; *Cos*, Rudolfo Hoyos; *Santa Ana*, David
Silva; *Travis*, William Hopper; *Austin*, Dayton Lummis;
Hockley, Nelson Leigh; *Baker*, Jody McCrea; *Deaf Smith*,
Chubby Johnson; *Sherman*, Roy Roberts; *Pepe*, Frank
Puglia; *Veramendi*, Salvador Baguez; *Crockett*, James
Griffith;

The idea of Joel McCrea as Sam Houston (1793-1863) was good, but unfortunately producer Walter Mirisch proceeded to film with a modest budget and the splendid scope necessary for telling the story of the first Governor of Texas was missing. Things might have been different if Mirisch had even half the money John Wayne had at his disposal in making *The Alamo* (1960). There had been other films touching upon this icon of Texas history, going back as far as 1917 when William Farnum played Houston in *The Conqueror*. Moroni Olsen was Houston in *Lone Star* (1952), Howard L. Negley played him in *The Last Command* (1955). However, the best treatment remains the one Republic made in 1939, *Man of Conquest*, with Richard Dix as Houston. That the McCrea version falls short is no fault of the actor.

It begins, as so many westerns, with a lonely figure slowly riding through beautiful western country. This figure happens to be Sam Houston, who has recently resigned as Governor of Tennessee for personal reasons and has moved to Texas to get away from politics and lead a quiet life. Those intentions are soon shunted aside by a body of Texas revolutionaries in this year of 1832. Houston, famous for his service as an officer under Andrew Jackson and as a successful governor, cannot hide his identity. The Texans want to free themselves from Mexican control and a group of them, headed by Jim Bowie (Jeff Morrow), Stephen Austin (Dayton Lummis) and Henry Delaney (Wallace Ford) urge Houston to be their leader. He declines, partly because he wants to marry Katherine Delaney (Felicia Farr), who does not want him involved.

Houston's mind is changed for him when President Jackson points out that it is vital for Texas to become independent and that its future lies with the United States. This request comes at a time when General Santa Ana (David Silva), known as "The Napoleon of the West," leads a revolution that gains him the Presidency of Mexico and a declaration from him that Texas be placed under martial law. William Travis (William Hopper) in San Antonio leads a force in repelling an attempted Mexican take-over, compelling the leaders of Texas to declare independence and draft a constitution, with Houston as Commander-in-Chief. Word reaches Houston that the Alamo in San Antonio has been overrun and all its defenders slaughtered by Santa Ana. Houston keeps adding to his numbers but continually moves away from Santa Ana rather than toward him, bringing criticism from his officers, with talk of cowardice. Then, when he is ready, Houston makes his stand. At the Battle of San Jacinto in 1936, he decisively defeats the Mexicans. Santa Ana is captured and Texas claims its independence. Katherine brings Houston the news that he has been declared the President of the Republic of Texas, the first Texan.

The First Texan cannot be faulted for its good intentions, only that producers have tried to do too much with too little. The production never matches the size and scope of its subject, and the film is weakened by trying to cover too wide a range of history, rather than focusing on the real drama, the events leading up to the Battle of San Jacinto. Also, while the love interest may be historically accurate, it seems somewhat contrived. McCrea, aided by the firm direction of the veteran Byron Haskins, emerges as a credible, dignified figure, but in a film that is so respectful, it tends to be almost antiseptic.

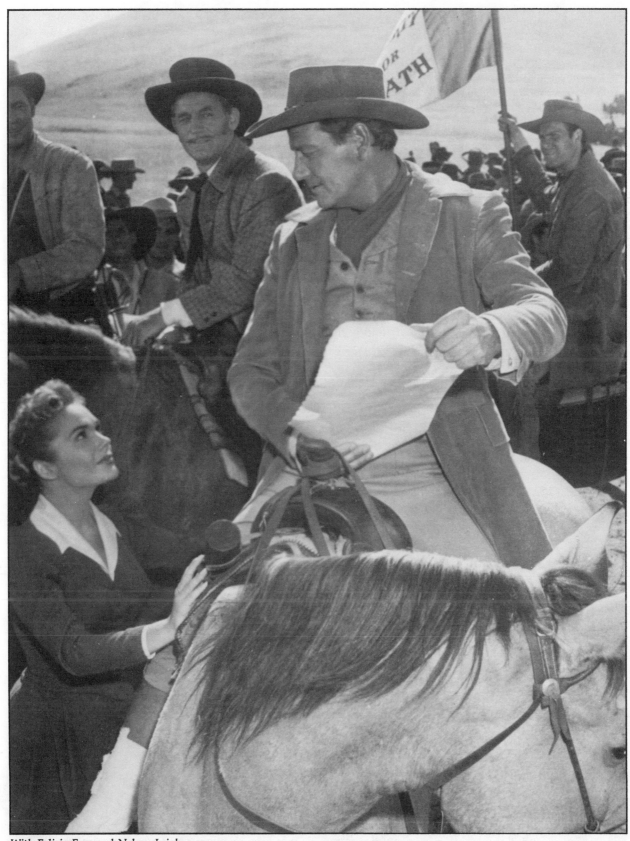

With Felicia Farr and Nelson Leigh.

THE OKLAHOMAN

Allied Artists, 1957;
Produced by Walter Mirisch; Directed by Francis D.
Lyon; Written by Daniel B. Ullman; Photographed in
Cinemascope and DeLuxe Color by Carl Guthrie; Music
by Hans Salter; 78 minutes.

Cast:
Dr. John Brighton, Joel McCrea; *Ann Barnes*, Barbara
Hale; *Cass Dobie*, Brad Dexter; *Maria Smith*, Gloria
Talbot; *Charlie Smith*, Michael Pate; *Jim Hawk*, Anthony
Caruso; *Mel Dobie*, Douglas Dick; *Mrs. Waynewright*,
Verna Felton; *Small Charlie*, Peter Votrian; *Bob Randall*,
Adam Williams; *Eliza*, Diane Brewster; *Marshall Bill*,
John Pickard; *Mrs. Fitzgerald*, Esther Dale; *Stableman*,
Ray Teal;

Joel McCrea's contract with Walter Mirisch called
for three films. As were the previous two, *The Oklahoman* was scripted by Daniel B. Ullman, although
along more modest lines than his accounts of Wyatt
Earp and Sam Houston. Here McCrea is John
Brighton, a doctor from Baltimore who decides in
1870 to move to California with his wife and daughter. As with so many other McCrea westerns, *The
Oklahoman* is about a peaceful man who reaches for
a gun only as a matter of last resort.

While traversing Oklahoma, Brighton loses his
wife in childbirth and rather than continue with his
friends to California, he decides to settle in the
nearby town of Cherokee Wells. He sets up practice
and rents accomodation from Mrs. Fitzgerald (Esther Dale), a kind-hearted lady who agrees to take
care of his daughter (Mimi Gibson) until Brighton
can find a place of his own. Next, he hires a pretty
young Indian girl, Maria (Gloria Talbot), as a house-
keeper and nanny. Maria is the daughter of farmer
Charlie Smith (Michael Pate), a gentle Cherokee
living in peace with his neighbors but well aware of
prejudice.

Brighton's life becomes more complicted for a
variety of reasons. He and widow rancher Anne
Barnes (Barbara Hale) become fond of each other,
with marriage appearing a fair assumption, until
Anne is disturbed by rumors that Maria is in love

With Gloria Talbot and Barbara Hale.

132

with her employer. The intimations of an affair between the doctor and the Indian girl are fanned by Cass Dobie (Brad Dexter), the most powerful rancher in the area and a man with whom Brighton has come into conflict. The doctor has had to patch up victims of Mel Dobie (Douglas Dick), the wild young brother of Cass.

The Dobies want to gain control of local farms and ranches, particularly that of Charlie Smith. The reason becomes obvious one night when Charlie shoots and kills Mel (Douglas Dick) as he prowls around a pond scooping samples into a bottle. Brighton comes to Charlie's defense and finds out that the pond shows evidence of containing oil. When Dobie comes to town to lead the lynching of

Charlie, Brighton finally straps on a gun and faces Dobie. In the shoot-out, the doctor is wounded, but Dobie dies, surprised as are the others that the gentle medico knows how to handle a revolver. Peace comes to Cherokee Wells and Anne comes to the side of the man she will marry.

The Oklahoman was too mild a western to thrill the kind of audience for which it was intended, but it is admirable for being one of the few to show the Cherokees as civilized people, living on farms, and touching upon the discovery of oil on their properties, which would eventually result in them becoming among the wealthiest of the tribes. For McCrea it was yet one more portrayal of the solid western citizen.

133

TROOPER HOOK

United Artists;
Produced by Sol Baer Fielding; Directed by Charles
Marquis Warren; Written by Charles Marquis Warren,
David Victor and Herbert Little, Jr., based on a story by
Jack Schaefer; Photographed by Ellsworth Fredericks;
Music by Gerald Fried; 81 minutes.

Cast:
Cora, Barbara Stanwyck; *Sergeant Hook*, Joel McCrea; *Jeff
Bennett*, Earl Holliman; *Fred Sutliff*, John Dehner; *Trude*,
Royal Dano; *Nanchez*, Rudolfo Acosta; *Charlie*, Edward
Andrews; *Consuela*, Susan Kohner; *Senora*, Celia Lovsky;
Quito, Terry Lawrence; *Salesman*, Stanley Adams; *Col.
Weaver*, Pat O'Moore; *Ann Weaver*, Jeanne Bates; *Corporal
Stoner*, Rush Williams; *Ryan*, Dick Shannon; *Tess*, D. J.
Thompson; *Cooter Brown*, Sheb Wooley;

Barbara Stanwyck was fifty in 1957, and as with
most lady stars of that age, major film roles ceased
to be plentiful. She appeared in only two films that
year, *Crime of Passion* with Sterling Hayden and
Trooper Hook, which brought her together with Joel
McCrea for the sixth and final time fifteen years
after *The Great Man's Lady*. Whereas, in previous
times Stanwyck had spoken up for McCrea, now

he, as an established superstar of westerns, was in a
position to ask for her. When producer Sol Baer
Fielding discussed leading ladies for this film - and
it is a film in which the lady is a major character -
McCrea had only one in mind. The screenplay directed by Charles Marquis Warren, who was also
the principle writer, is about a woman captured by
Indians, and forced to live as a squaw. That theme
had been dealt with by John Ford in both *The
Searchers* (1955) and *Two Rode Together* (1961), but in
neither case did Ford have an actress as powerful as
Stanwyck.

Photographed in stark black-and-white in the
Arizona desert country south of Tucson by
Ellsworth Fredericks, *Trooper Hook* tells of a cavalry
sergeant (McCrea) who leads his squad in razing
the village of a cruel Apache, Nanchez (Rudolfo
Acosta), as a reprisal for raids on settlers. Among
the squaws Hook finds a white woman, Cora (Stanwyck), in company with her five-year-old son Quito
(Terry Lawrence), the child of Nanchez. Hook takes
them to his post, from where Cora decides to leave
to seek her husband, Fred Sutliff (John Dehner),
who owns a ranch near Tucson.

Hook is assigned to take Cora to the ranch, and
enroute she gets some idea of the problems she
faces with an Indian child. The boy's life is threat-

With Rudolfo Acosta.

ened by various bullies and at one stop the manager of a hotel refuses to feed them. Only the sympathetic understanding of Hook makes the long ride by stagecoach bearable. During the trip they learn that Nanchez is after them, intent on reclaiming his son. To avoid a possible ambush, Hook orders the stage to drive across open country but it overturns when it hits a rock. Soon Nanchez arrives with a dozen warriors. Under a flag of truce he offers safe conduct for all in return for Quito. Hook refuses but he bluffs Nanchez from attacking by threatening to kill the boy if he does.

The stage is allowed to proceed to Sutliff's ranch, where he shocks Cora by refusing to accept the boy. Cora then asks Hook to drive her to Tucson. Sutliff draws his gun and forbids her to leave, moments before Nanchez and his warriors swoop down on the ranch. As Hook drives a wagon from the ranch

with Cora and Quito, Sutliff jumps in, and in the running battle both he and Nanchez are killed. With their chief dead the Apaches break off the fight, leaving Cora and her son free to look forward to a life with the compassionate cavalry sergeant.

While far from being a great western, *Trooper Hook* is a good one, largely because of the acting of McCrea and Stanwyck. *The New York Times* reviewer commented, "Armed with some good, blunt dialogue, Miss Stanwyck and Mr. McCrea deliver a pair of easy, restrained, natural performances typical of two screen veterans. Is anyone surprised?"

About Barbara Stanwyck, who died in January of 1990 at the age of eighty-two, McCrea said, "She was, with no reservations, the best I ever met. Every crew we ever worked with loved and admired her and so did I. She taught me a lot and I shall be ever grateful to her."

With Barbara Stanwyck and Terry Lawrence.

GUNSIGHT RIDGE

United Artists, 1957;
Produced by Robert Bassler; Directed by Francis D.
Lyon; Written by Talbot and Elizabeth Jennings;
Photographed by Ernest Laszlo; Music by David
Raksin; 85 minutes.

Cast:
Mike Ryan, Joel McCrea; *Velvet,* Mark Stevens; *Molly,*
Joan Weldon; *Rosa,* Darlene Fields; *Sheriff Jones,*
Addison Richards; *Girl,* Carolyn Craig; *Babcock,* Robert
Griffin; *Hank Moss,* Slim Pickens; *Daggett,* Stanford
Jolley; *Gus Withers,* George Chandler; *Justice,* Herb
Vigran; *Bride,* Cindy Robbins; *Groom,* Jody McCrea;
Ramon, Martin Garralaga;

The next producer to approach Joel McCrea was
Robert Bassler, who had bought *Gunsight Ridge,* an
original screenplay written by Talbot Jennings and
his wife Elizabeth. While the plot about the conflict
between a Wells Fargo agent and a crook stealing
from that company was fairly conventional, Mc-
Crea was impressed with the characterizations of
the antagonists. His role, that of Mike Ryan, allowed for a lot more humor and a lighter touch than
he was usually offered. The villain had the intriguing name of Velvet Clark, a stylish mine owner who
also plays the piano. The role of the villain was

offered to Mark Stevens, then a star in his own
right, who probably welcomed the chance to get
away from playing heroes.

In *Gunsight Ridge* the plot is meager and the
playing is everything. Mike Ryan is assigned the
task of finding out who is holding up stagecoaches
and taking gold shipments emanating from the
mines, robberies that also involve many killings.
Ryan discovers that the man behind it all is Velvet
Clark, but it is difficult to prove the charges because
Clark is a respected mine owner who covers his
tracks rather neatly. When the town sheriff (Addison Richards) finds evidence of Clark's operation,
Clark kills him. The sheriff's daughter Molly (Joan
Weldon), who is fond of Ryan, encourages him to
take over her father's job. Now, as a lawman, Ryan
keeps after Clark until he has all he needs to bring
about the shoot-out that costs Clark his life. With
the case solved Ryan settles down and marries
Molly.

Gunsight Ridge is not among the best of the Mc-
Crea Westerns but it did give him a chance to appear a little less sobersided than several other such
roles. While the part is still that of the quietly determined hero, here he has lines that allow him to
reveal his sense of timing and comedic instincts that
men like Preston Sturges and George Stevens long
ago spotted.

With Herb Vigran, Jody McCrea, and Cindy Robbins.

With Mark Stevens.

THE TALL STRANGER

Allied Artists, 1957;
Produced by Walter Mirisch; Directed by Thomas Carr;
Written by Christopher Knopf, based on the story
Showdown Trail (later retitled *Plunder*) by Louis
L'Amour; Photographed in Cinemascope and DeLuxe
Color by Wilfred Cline; Music by Hans Salter; 83
minutes.

Cast:
Ned Bannon, Joel McCrea; *Ellen*, Virginia Mayo; *Bishop*,
Barry Kelley; *Zarata*, Michael Ansara; *Judson*, Whit
Bissell; *Dud*, James Dobson; *Harper*, George Neise; *Red*,
Adam Kennedy; *Charley*, Michael Pate; *Stark*, Leo
Gordon; *Cap*, Ray Teal; *Will*, Philip Phillips; *Pagones*,
Robert Foulk; *Mary*, Jenifer Lee; *Chavez*, George J.
Lewis;

Joel McCrea signed a second contract with Walter Mirisch in 1957 to do another three westerns. The first of these, *The Tall Stranger*, paired him with Virginia Mayo, eight years after their fine work together in *Colorado Territory*. However, this one would not be in the same league with that Raoul Walsh-directed western. On the credit side is a good screenplay by Christopher Knopf, based on a Louis L'Armour story, a goodly amount of action amid splendid scenery shot in DeLuxe Color and Cinemascope by Wally Cline, and a lively music score by the veteran Viennese-born composer Hans Salter. Salter had already scored three McCrea westerns, *Frenchie*, *Whichita* and *The Oklahoman*, and would score the upcoming *Gunfight in Dodge City*. In the hands of veteran craftsmen like McCrea, Cline and Salter, no western was likely to be a bad one.

The Tall Stranger again transports McCrea back to the immediate post-Civil War years, although this time as a Union Army veteran. Ned Bannon (McCrea) has traveled west to join his half-brother Bishop (Barry Kelly), who owns a big ranch in Bishop Valley, California. As Bannon draws near his destination he is shot from ambush, badly wounded and left to die. Before losing consciousness, he sees a man wearing fancy riding boots and carrying a nickle-plated rifle. Some time later, a wagon party made up of immigrants from the distressed South come by and pick up Bannon. The train is led by Harper (George Neise) and it includes Ellen (Mayo) and her young son. She claims to be a widow and she nurses Bannon back to health.

Bannon soon realizes that something is amiss. He warns the travelers that they are being led astray by Harper, who is in league with Mexican renegade Zarata (Michael Ansara) to kill Bishop and take over his property. It also turns out that it was Zarata who shot Bannon. Harper has intended to use the settlers as a means of infiltrating Bishop Valley, but those plans are thwarted by Bannon. Harper, Zarata and their men now besiege Bishop in a battle that costs them their lives, along with that of Bishop, who strangles Zarata before expiring. Bannon, the land now his, opens it to the settlers, which includes Ellen as Mrs. Bannon. She has confessed that she was never married but simply looking for a new life for herself and her son. She finds it.

As the reviewer for *Variety* noted, McCrea, "who knows his way around a western script, enacts the hero with customary authority and conviction." In the hands of producer Mirisch, he also had plenty of help. *The Tall Stranger* reflects some of the changing production codes coming into effect by 1957. The dialogue includes cuss words like "damn" and "hell," and there are references to illegitimacy, rape and houses of prostitution. In a few years this would be mild stuff, but at the time it marked a slightly more mature attitude, especially in westerns.

With Virginia Mayo.

CATTLE EMPIRE

20th Century-Fox, 1958;
Produced by Robert Stabler; Directed by Charles Marquis Warren; Written by Endre Bohem and Eric Norden, based on a story by Danile B. Ullman; Photographed in Cinemascope and DeLuxe Color by Brydon Baker; Music by Paul Sawtell and Bert Shefter; 82 minutes.

Cast:
John Cord, Joel McCrea; *Sandy,* Gloria Talbot; *Ralph Hamilton,* Don Haggerty; *Janice Hamilton,* Phyllis Coates; *Douglas Hamilton,* Bing Russell; *Tom Jeffrey,* Paul Brinegar; *George Jeffrey,* Hal K. Dawson; *Aruzza,* Duane Gray; *Garth,* Richard Shannon; *Tom Powis,* Charles Gray; *Cogswell,* Patrick O'Moore; *Jim Whittaker,* William McGraw; *Sheriff Brewster,* Jack Lomas; *Corbo,* Steve Raines; *Quince,* Rocky Shaham; *Barkeep,* Neadon Booth; *Grainger,* Bill Hale; *Stitch,* Ronald Foster; *Preacher,* Howard B. Culver;

Cattle Empire has the most unusual opening of any Joel McCrea western. The actor is lying in the street of a grubby western town, his hands tied together at the end of a rope, and he is then dragged by a man on a galloping horse as on lookers express their loud approval. John Cord (McCrea) has just been released after five years in jail and has re-

turned to the town in which he was arrested. The citizens are taking their revenge on Cord for allowing his trail herders to drunkenly shoot up the town, causing death, injury and damage. Now, after several draggings the cut and battered Cord is in danger of losing his own life.

The man who stops the abuse is Ralph Hamilton (Don Haggerty), after whom the town is named. Hamilton is blind as a result of the melee five years earlier, but he now offers Cord a job, to the puzzlement of the citizens. He appreciates Cord's ability as a trail boss and needs him to drive a large herd of his cattle to the army, a sale that will bring back some prosperity to the run-down town. Cord accepts, but with a measure of bitterness. Hamilton has married Janice (Phyllis Coates), the girl to whom he was once engaged. Partly out of spite, but also for the money, Cord accepts a second job as trail boss to Hamilton's rival, Garth (Richard Shannon), who also wants to sell his herd to the army. Cord acts as an advisor to Garth, setting him off three days ahead of the Hamilton herd.

Once under way, Cord shuttles back and forth between the two herds, with his emotional dilemma made worse by Hamilton's young sister Sandy (Gloria Talbot) falling in love with him. Cord warns Garth to avoid going in the direction of a river that he knows has dried up, but Garth ignores the ad-

With Paul Brinegar and Hal K. Dawson.

140

FORT MASSACRE

United Artists, 1958;
Produced by Walter Mirisch; Directed by Joseph M. Newman; Written by Martin M. Goldsmith; Photographed in Cinemascope and DeLuxe Color by Carl Guthrie; Music by Marlin Skiles; 80 minutes.

Cast:
Sergeant Vinson, Joel McCrea; *McGurney,* Forrest Tucker; *Piute Girl,* Susan Cabot; *Travis,* John Russell; *Pawnee,* Anthony Caruso; *Schwabacker,* Bob Osterloh; *Collins,* Denver Pyle; *Pendleton,* George W. Neise; *Moss,* Rayford Barnes; *Tucker,* Guy Prescott; *Moving Cloud,* Larry Chance; *Charlie,* Irving Bacon; *Adele,* Claire Carleton; *Piute Man,* Francis J. McDonald; *Chief,* Charles Kray;

With *Fort Massecre* Walter Mirisch launched his new company, The Mirisch Corporation, and switched his releasing outlet from Allied Artists to the much more powerful United Artists. It offered Joel McCrea a character vastly different from his usual staunch westerner. In this one, he is a veteran cavalry sergeant named Vinson, a man festering with bitterness. It is by far the most grim role Mc-Crea ever played.

As the film opens a detachment of cavalry moves across the Arizona desert. It is attacked by Apaches

With John Russell.

vice and his herd comes to a standstill for lack of water. Garth comes after Cord, convinced that Cord was responsible for his problem. In the meantime, Hamilton's men have turned on Cord, and he is saved only by the admission from Hamilton that it was he and Garth who were responsible for the shooting up of the town five years before, and not Cord. Cord leads the Hamilton men in repulsing the Garth attack, and in the ensuing conflict, Hamilton dies and Garth is captured. Afterwards the citizens ask Cord to stay in town. He says he first needs to go elsewhere and find a place of his own; then he will come back to get Sandy.

Cattle Empire is good strong stuff, with McCrea a little more dour than usual, understandable in view of the physical abuse and contempt levied against the man portrayed. Credit is due director Charles Marquis Warren, then among the most respected of western writers. It was Warren who was the principle director of the successful television series *Gunsmoke.*

141

With Russell and Susan Cabott.

With Anthony Caruso, Rayford Barnes, and Forrest Tucker.

and several men die, including the officer, which leaves Vinson in command. A hard, tough soldier, he is not popular among the survivors, who question the short route he has chosen in order to get back to their post. The route requires passage through restricted Apache territory and the men suspect that Vinson's reasons are personal. They are. Vinson's wife and two children were slaughtered by Apaches and he is half-crazed with revenge. He deliberately provokes an Apache attack, which he skillfully defeats, but when the leader offers to surrender, Vinson kills him in cold blood, to the disgust of his men.

Only a half dozen soldiers survive the battle with the Indians, and only one of them, an educated private named Travis (John Russell), has any understanding of Vinson's state of mind. After moving through more hostile territory, the group holes up in old Indian cave dwelling, which the men dub Fort Massacre, realizing that is what it is likely to become for them as the Apaches close in. In the abandoned dwellings they find an elderly Indian (Francis J. McDonald) and a young Indian girl (Susan Cabot). She helps the soldiers by lying to the attacking Apaches about the presence of the men, but as the Apaches withdraw, Vinson cannot resist

With Barnes, Russell, and Caruso.

THE GUNFIGHT AT DODGE CITY

United Artists, 1959;
Produced by Walter Mirisch; Directed by Joseph M. Newman; Written by Danile B. Ullman and Martin M. Goldsmith; Photographed in Cinemascope and DeLuxe Color by Carl Guthrie; Music by Hans Salter; 81 minutes.

Cast:
Bat Masterson, Joel McCrea; *Pauline*, Julie Adams; *Doc*, John McIntire; *Lily*, Nancy Gates; *Dave*, Richard Anderson; *Rev. Howard*, Jim Westerfield; *Ben*, Walter Coy; *Regan*, Don Haggerty; *Billy*, Wright King; *Ed*, Harry Lauter; *Forbes*, Myron Healy; *Purley*, Maurice Hugo; *Bartender*, Henry Kulkey;

Westerns have seldom touched upon reality, especially as it pertains to the pain and misery involved in fighting with guns. For this reason the opening scene of *Gunfight at Dodge City* is a virtual aberation from the fiction concocted for films of this kind. Playing the legendary lawman Bat Masterson, Joel McCrea is asked by a youngster, "Mr. Masterson, what's it like...to kill a man?" Masterson muses for a moment and glumly replies:

"First, you're facing him, and you're plenty scared. You want to run - anywhere - to hide. But

firing upon them. More soldiers die until only three are left, including Vinson and Travis. As they are about to leave after beating off the Apaches, Vinson turns his gun on the old Indian with the intention of killing him. Instead it is Vinson who dies from a shot fired by Travis, who cannot tolerate the senseless killing, but who also know there is nothing left for Vinson.

Fort Massacre was not a successful film, possibly being a little too grim as entertainment. But it is an interesting picture for those who study the Indian wars between the Army and the Apaches in the 1870's. It pulls no punches in showing the brutal conditions of the time and place, and it offered McCrea his most unusual western role. It is a study of the deterioration of a man's character under the stress and strain of the responsibility of command and the pressure of attack. The role of Vinson was the closest McCrea ever came to playing a villain and the plausibility of the role was a credit to him.

144

With John McIntire.

you can't, because if you make even the smallest move he's bound to draw. So you watch his eyes and you're praying he'll back down and say something that'll give you a chance to get out of it. Then you try to make yourself say something. But before you can, it's too late. He's on the floor - and the cuspidor's spilled - and people buy you drinks and say he drew first. But you're seeing that thing on the floor that ten seconds ago was a man and now is just a lump - and you wonder why it all happened - and you go out back where no one will see you, and vomit..."

Unfortunately nothing else in *Gunfight at Dodge City* matches the reality and the wisdom revealed in this opening sequence. The script by Daniel B. Ullman and Martin M. Goldsmith attempts to deviate from the norm in telling the conventional story of a reluctant lawman bringing peace to an outlaw infested town. The fact that McCrea appears as Bat Masterson has no real historical validity in this film;

he is simply an actor playing a role he and so many others have played before under any number of names.

The Ullman-Goldsmith script has Masterson fleeing Hays City, Kansas, after killing a soldier in a saloon. Although done in self defense, he deems it better to run than explain. He goes to Dodge City, where his brother Ed (Harry Lauter) is the sheriff trying to get re-elected in the face of opposition from the crime faction. Masterson's reputation with a gun and his love of gambling does not endear him to the reformers who back his brother, especially Ed's prudish fiancée Pauline (Julie Adams). Masterson buys a half interest in a saloon with Lily (Nancy Gates), but when Ed is killed, Masterson accepts the invitation to run for sheriff. Under his tough leadership trouble in Dodge City begins to ebb, which wins him the affection of Pauline.

Trouble for Masterson rears up when the retarded son of his friend Ben (Walter Coy) is arrested for a killing, with a probable hanging as punishment. Masterson agrees with Ben that the boy should be hospitalized rather than executed, and in collusion with a doctor (John McIntire), he arranges to get the boy out of town. Having violated the law, Masterson is now a wanted man. However, rather than flee, he decides to face Regan (Don Haggerty), the man he now knows was responsible for his brother's death. In the inevitable battle between the two men, Masterson survives. This reinstates him in the eyes of the citizens but not the snooty Pauline. Masterson realizes that the warm Lily is the one for him.

Somehow all the parts of *Gunfight at Dodge City* do not add up to a satisfying whole. The plot lines are a little too complicated and the material, except for the arresting opening scene, far too familiar. An accurate account of the fabled Bat Masterson would have served McCrea much better, especially in view of the fancified one then being presented in the popular television series starring Gene Barry. There are moments in this film in which McCrea shows some of his skill with light comedy but they are not enough. The pity is that McCrea was never able to make a western spoof. He might have been marvelous.

WICHITA TOWN

NBC-TV, 1950

After completing his contract with the Mirisch company for the three feature films, Joel McCrea declined to sign another such contract. Walter Mirisch changed his tactic and suggested to McCrea that they do a television series, one that would be something of a spin-off from the successful film *Wichita*. McCrea liked the idea, especially when it was agreed that his son Jody would be the co-star. The result was *Wichita Town*, a weekly half-hour that started its run on NBC in September of 1959.

In *Wichita Town*, McCrea appeared as Marshall Mike Dunbar, who with his deputy Ben Matheson (Jody), attends to the law and order in Wichita, Kansas, in the years following the Civil War. The series began with Dunbar arriving in Whichita after having led a cattle drive from Texas, followed by the decision to settle in the town and become its marshall. With the lawlessness of the territory at that time, the writers of the series had plenty of

material from which to draw, although it turned out to be little different from what western fans had long watched in countless films and other TV series.

Wichita Town had two strikes against it. First, it appeared at a time when the airwaves were glutted with westerns, including the very popular *Gunsmoke* and *Bonanza*. Second, NBC broadcast it from 10:30 to 11:00 PM, always a difficult timeslot for a series; also the fact that it ran only 30 minutes was a possible negative factor. Only twenty-four episodes were made, and these were repeated between June and September of 1960.

Ironically, it was one of the few television series ever to go on the air without first having been tested in pilot form. NBC was so confident of success, based on the reputation of McCrea and Mirisch, that the series was accepted in concept form. All parties involved were very disappointed with the reception. McCrea had considered retirement after making *Gunfight at Dodge City*, and after *Wichita Town* there was little doubt in his mind.

RIDE THE HIGH COUNTRY

MGM, 1961;
Produced by Richard E. Lyons; Directed by Sam
Peckenpah; Written by N. B. Stone, Jr.
Photographed in Metrocolor by Lucien Ballard; Music
by George Bassman; 93 minutes.

Cast:
Gil Westrum, Randolph Scott; *Steve Judd*, Joel McCrea;
Heck Longtree, Ronald Starr; *Elsa Knudsen*, Mariette
Hartley; *Billy Hammond*, James Drury; *Joshua Knudsen*,
R. G. Armstrong; *Judge Tolliver*, Edgar Buchanan; *Kate*,
Jennie Jackson; *Elder Hammond*, John Anderson; *Sylvus
Hammond*, L. Q. Jones; *Henry Hammond*, Warren Oates;
Jimmy Hammond, John Davis Chandler;

Gunfight at Dodge City was released in May of
1959. In March of the following year came *Comanche
Station*, starring Randolph Scott. Like McCrea, Scott
had decided that it was time to retire from the
picture business. Both had been on the screen for
over thirty years and both had decided to specialize
in westerns in the latter years of their careers. Also,
they were both very wealthy gentlemen. It would
take something of unusual interest to get them to
labor before the movie cameras again.

Burt Kennedy, who had written *Comanche Station*
and three other stylish westerns that Scott had
made with director Budd Boetticher, sent Scott a
story he found fascinating, *Guns in the Afternoon* by
N. B. Stone, Jr. It told of a pair of impoverished,
over-the-hill former lawmen getting together on a
job. Scott liked the concept. It had an elegiac quality
about it, dealing with men past their prime and
their time, one man honorbound and the other embittered and pragmatic. He agreed to do it if Kennedy and producer Richard E. Lyon, could get
McCrea.

McCrea's reaction to the proposal of working
with Scott was positive, except that he did not care
too much for Lyons' suggestion that he play Gil
Westrum, the man who sees a chance to make some
easy money, even if it means turning on the un-
bending, moral Steve Judd. "Lyons thought I was a
little more subtle than Randy and that it would be a
little more deceptive if I would turn and double-
cross him. But I told him that if I was going to make
one more picture, I wasn't going to destroy my
image with it. My image was Steve Judd. He's the
guy, through his integrity, will get the job done. I

asked Lyons not to say anything to Randy because
he was the guy who came up with the project and
ought to have a choice about which man he would
play. But if he chose Judd, I'd back out. We all had
lunch at the Brown Derby, along with Sam Peckinpah, who was going to direct, and I put it to Randy.
He said he'd play either one but if he had the choice
he'd prefer Westrum. He said, 'I've played the
straight, honest guy so damn long and so much that
this would be interesting.' I told him that was fine
by me because I wanted to play Judd."

When MGM released *Ride the High Country* - the
original title *Guns in the Afternoon* was retained for
the British release - it did so with little promotion,
thinking it too offbeat a western to win much of an
audience. To the studio's amazement film critics
lavished praise upon it. *Newsweek* named it the best
film of 1962, as did the editor of the prestigious *Film
Quarterly*, and it won a prize at the Venice Film
Festival. Since then, it has appeared on the favored
film list of just about every western film buff. Even
without Scott and McCrea it would be an interesting story; with them it is a special film in which two
giants of the genre appear to summarize their long
association with western film.

Ride the High Country is about a pair of middle-
aged westerners washed aside by civilization in the
turn-of-the-century West; two once heroic men now
reduced to picking up a living as best they can.
Judd rides into the town of Hornitos to take a job
escorting gold shipments from the mining community of Course Gold. He does his best to hide his
frayed shirtcuffs when applying for the job and he
goes into the toilet to read his contract so that the
hiring banker cannot see his need for glasses. He
needs an assistant in order to do the job, and while
walking around town bumps into Westrum, an old
friend, who is now making a living as a sideshow
sharpshooter spouting Buffalo Bill nonsense about
the Wild West. Westrum agrees to come in with
Judd but insists on bringing in his young, scrap-
happy friend Heck Longtree (Ronald Starr). Despite
their long friendship and their work together as
lawmen, Judd and Westrum are different kinds of
men. Judd abides by his ironclad code of honor,
whereas Westrum sees the job as a chance to steal
gold as recompense for all his years of underpaid
law service.

On their way through the mountains - the film
was shot in the California Sierras in the area of Lake
Mammoth - the men stop at the home of Joshua
Knudsen (R. G. Armstrong), a farmer and religious
fanatic. Heck takes a shine to Knudsen's repressed

With Ron Starr and Randolph Scott.

With Randolph Scott.

149

With Randolph Scott.

daughter Elsa (Mariette Hartley). Simply to escape home, Elsa had accepted a marriage proposal from miner Billy Hammond (James Drury), one of five brothers living in Coarse Gold. Judd and Westrum reluctantly agree to take Elsa to Hammond, but when she gets to her intended husband she is disgusted to fine the Hammonds a wild and filthy bunch living in squalor. She goes through with the wedding, which takes place in a saloon-bordello, but then, with Billy drunk, she has to fight off the other brothers who seem to regard her as communal property. Realizing her plight, Judd and Westrum agree to take her back to her father. This sets up a conflict with the Hammonds, who not only want Elsa, but the gold as well. In their first attack, two of the brothers are killed, but now Judd finds himself with an additional problem on his hands - Westrum also wants the gold. Judd ties Westrum's hands behind his back and Heck, because of his love for Elsa, sides with Judd. Westrum escapes during the night and goes back to the scene of the

fight with the Hammonds, where he finds a rifle and a horse.

When Judd gets to the Knudsen ranch he finds the old man has been murdered and that the three remaining Hammond brothers are holed up in the barn. A gunfight erupts and Judd and Heck are wounded, and Westrum, who has been following them from a distance, rides down to join his old friend. As they lie in a ditch, they agree that the best tactic is to challenge the Hammonds to an open fight. With insulting taunts they bring the brothers into the open, their guns blazing away. Judd and Westrum stand, aim carefully and bring down the Hammonds. In the exchange Judd receives two more bullets. He knows it is over for him and he tells Westrum to take Elsa and Heck away because he does not want them to see him die, "I'll go it alone." Westrum assures him, "Don't worry about anything, I'll take care of it." Says Judd, "Hell, I know that, I always did. You just forget it for a while, that's all. So long, partner." Then as the oth-

With Scott.

ers ride away, Judd muses for a moment, closes his eyes, slowly lies back and dies.

No western has ever dealt with morality more surely than *Ride the High Country*. When Westrum pleads with Judd to join him in taking the gold shipment, saying, "The bankers won't be hurt by the loss," Judd angrily replies, "No, not them, only *me*!" And in discussing the rigid morality of her bible-bound, widower father, the puzzled Elsa asks, "My father says there's only right and wrong, good and evil, nothing in between. It isn't that simple, it it?" Replies Judd, "No, it isn't. It should be, but it isn't."

The major assets of *Ride the High Country* are clearly Joel McCrea and Randolph Scott, both of whom had help form a dignified style of mythic western heroism in the movies. For Scott it represented complete retirement. For the remaining twenty-seven years of his life - he died in 1988 at ninety - he had nothing more to do with Hollywood. He was the only actor accepted as a member of the elite Los Angeles Country Club, which rightly regarded him as an astute business tycoon and one of the unpublicized sponsors of the Mayo Clinic. Scott was in fact one of the wealthiest men in the film community, having invested wisely and having managed his business interests with a sure hand. It is perhaps somewhat ironic that both he and McCrea, also wealthy, appear in *Ride the High Country* as a pair of poverty stricken has-beens. In reality nothing could have been further from the truth.

With Scott.

152

With Scott and Starr.

With Scott, Starr, and Mariette Hartley.

153

With Randolph Scott.

154

CRY BLOOD, APACHE

Golden Eagle Goldstone, 1970;
Produced by Jody McCrea and Harold Roberts;
Directed by Jack Starrett; Written by Sean MacGregor,
based on a story by Harold Roberts; Photographed in
color by Bruce Scott; Music by Elliot Kaplan; 82
minutes.

Cast:
Pitcalin (young man), Jody McCrea; *Vittorio*, Dan Kemp;
Jemmo, Marie Gahva; *Benji*, Rick Nervick; *Two Card*,
Robert Tessier; *Dracon*, Jack Starrett; *Cochalla*, Carolyn
Stellar; *Old Indian*, Carroll Kemp; *Mother*, Barbara
Sanford; *Pitcalin (old man)*, Joel McCrea;

Joel McCrea did not appear in another film for
nine years after *Ride the High Country*, and sadly,
when he finally did, it would be one in which very
few people would be aware of his presence. In 1970,
his son Jody, who had played small roles in a number of films, formed a production partnership
with Harold Roberts to make what they hoped

would be an adult western, *Cry Blood, Apache*. With
Jody playing the lead as a young prospector named
Pitcalin, it was fairly easy to ask father Joel to make
a token appearance to give weight to the project.
McCrea senior appears at the beginning and at the
end of the film, playing Pitcalin forty years later
when he revisits the scene of a harrowing experience from his youth.

The story is told in a flashback. It opens with an
older Pitcalin (Joel McCrea) riding up to the rem-
nents of an old campground. As he looks around, he
remembers an incident from many years ago. As a
young man, Pitcalin, with three other prospectors,
comes across a small band of Apaches who knew the
location of a gold mine. When the idians refuse to
reveal the location of the mine, the quartet kills all
the Indians except for a girl (Marie Gahva) whom
Pitcalin protects. After the attacks of Apaches seek-
ing revenge and the lethal arguments between the
prospectors, only Pitcalin is left alive. As a much
older man Pitcalin reflects on all this trauma and
horror, muses for a while and then rides away.

With Jody McCrea.

With a muddled plot and a cast of unsympathetic characters, *Cry Blood, Apache* failed to win many bookings and soon drifted into film oblivion, taking with it Jody McCrea's last major stab at a film career.

MUSTANG COUNTRY

Universal, 1976;
Produced, directed and written by John Champion;
Photographed in Technicolor by J. Barry Herron; Music by Lee Holdridge; 79 minutes.

Cast:
Dan, Joel McCrea; *Griff*, Robert Fuller; *Tee Jay*, Patrick Wayne; *Nika*, Nika Mina;

Many scripts were sent to Joel McCrea after *Ride the High Country* but none of them moved him to accept. "The things that had been submitted to me were not very interesting or exciting, and most of them were on the degrading level, which I didn't ever want to do because I had kind of established an image, such as it was. I saw no reason to become an anti-hero."

The film that managed to get McCrea back was not one that originated in Hollywood. Young Canadian writer-director John Champion contacted McCrea to say that he not only wanted the actor to play the lead in his story *Mustang Country*, but that he could get backing from Universal if McCrea would agree. McCrea liked the script and after meeting Champion and finding him likeable he told Universal to go ahead with the arrangements. Part of the attraction for McCrea was that the entire film would be shot in Banff National Park, Alberta, Canada. The story was about a horse, an old cowboy and a young Indian boy. Nothing degrading or sleazy.

The story is set in 1925, along the Alberta-Montana border and tells about a small-time rancher and former rodeo champion named Dan (McCrea) who sets out to capture a wild black stallion, a mustang known as Shoshone. Two younger cowboys (Patrick Wayne and Robert Fuller) rope the horse but lose him after a chase and give up. Dan also catches up with Shoshone but ends up

156

With Nika Mina.

tossed in a river attempting to rope him. An Indian lad, Mika (Mika Mina), an orphan who has run away from school, comes across Dan and joins him in the search for the horse. Mika wants to earn some money to give to his only living relative, his grandmother. Their attempts to capture the horse end in frustration as the wily animal outsmarts them until Shoshone comes to the aid of Dan's horse Rosey when it is stuck in a mud-filled gully. With the stallion in hand Dan goes back to his ranch with Mika, telling the boy he now has a home.

The plot of *Mustang Country* is paper thin, and despite all the beautiful scenery and the well staged sequences with horses, dogs and bears the film failed to find either good critical response of much of a market. More is the pity because for those who enjoy animals and the scenic outdoor it is a pleasant film to watch. McCrea claimed that it was a pleasure to make, indeed something of a vacation for he, his wife and their camera-enthusiast son Peter, and that the physical work called for was no problem for him. At the age of seventy McCrea was still riding every day on his own ranch. The only difficulty after fifteen years away from the picture business was learning the script. "I wasn't as quick a study as I had been. I had to think about it, but the rest of it was just like before."

The reviewer for *Variety*, writing under the byline Mack, seemed to strike the concensus in regarding *Mustang Country* rather bland entertainment, although he made some good points about the star: "McCrea's particular strength as a western actor has always been the serenity of his character, an unflappable, straight-as-an-arrow rectitude beautifully displayed in his previous film, Sam Peckipah's *Ride the High Country*, and in other top oaters such as *Stars in My Crown*, *Wichita*, and *Buffalo Bill*." The reviewer added that although audiences of children might enjoy *Mustange Country*, "those who remember McCrea's finer moments will hope he doesn't go back to the ranch and let this film be his valedictory."

For better or for worse *Mustang Country* turned out to be Joel McCrea's valedictory. No one after 1976 was able to get him off the ranch and into a studio or a film location. He decided that his eighty films made over a period of forty-six years was enough.

A personal footnote: A few years ago I wrote a screenplay I titled *Old Soldier*, the story of a long retired cavalry officer who is tricked by crooks into becoming part of a scam to rob ranchers. In my mind's eys I could see Joel McCrea playing my old soldier. I telephoned him and outlined the story, which he seemed to like. I then found the courage to ask, "May I send you the script?" There was a pause, "No. Better not. I might like it." Like so many others, I too had failed to get Joel McCrea back into the picture business.

Joel McCrea and Francis Dee (Mr. & Mrs. Joel McCrea).

158